THE MAGIC OF MIDDLE SCHOOL MUSICALS

Inspire Your Students to Learn, Grow, and Succeed

Victor V. Bobetsky

Published in partnership with
MENC: The National Association for Music Education
Frances S. Ponick, Executive Editor

Rowman & Littlefield Education
Lanham • New York • Toronto • Plymouth, UK

Published in partnership with
MENC: The National Association for Music Education

Published in the United States of America
by Rowman & Littlefield Education
A Division of Rowman & Littlefield Publishers, Inc.
A wholly owned subsidary of The Rowman & Littlefield Publishing Group, Inc.
4501 Forbes Boulevard, Suite 200, Lanham, Maryland 20706
www.rowmaneducation.com

Estover Road
Plymouth PL6 7PY
United Kingdom

British Library Cataloguing in Publication Information Available

Library of Congress Cataloging-in-Publication Data

Bobetsky, Victor V.
    The magic of middle school musicals : inspire your students to learn, grow,
and succeed / Victor V. Bobetsky.
        p.   cm.
    "Published in partnership with MENC, the National Association for Music
Education."
    Includes bibliographical references.
    ISBN-13: 978-1-57886-867-4 (cloth : alk. paper)
    ISBN-10: 1-57886-867-X (cloth : alk. paper)
    ISBN-13: 978-1-57886-868-1 (pbk. : alk. paper)
    ISBN-10: 1-57886-868-8 (pbk. : alk. paper)
    eISBN-13: 978-1-57886-981-7
    eISBN-10: 1-57886-981-1
    1. Musicals—Juvenile—Production and direction.   I. Title.
MT955.B575   2008
792.602'26—dc22
2008032795

This book is dedicated to the memory of my parents,
Victor and Marie L. Bobetsky

CONTENTS

FOREWORD

I am very pleased to write the foreword to this much needed contribution to the profession, *The Magic of Middle School Musicals: Inspire Your Students to Learn, Grow, and Succeed*, by Victor V. Bobetsky. Pedagogical texts in music education often neglect the unique needs of middle school students and teachers. This book is a step-by-step guide to planning, rehearsing, producing, and performing musicals at the middle school level. It provides useful information for you and your students about every aspect of this endeavor, from finding an appropriate show or creating an original musical to auditions, casting, staging, and assessment.

You'll learn strategies for arranging music for middle school voices, teaching the music to your students, creating choreography, and dealing with the logistics involved in a real school setting for rehearsals and performances.

A musical, by its very nature, requires a collaborative approach. This book shows you how to work effectively with your fellow teachers and how to garner parental, school, and community support for the production and for your program.

You'll find this book to be a valuable resource whether you've had experience with musicals or, perhaps more importantly, if you've had little or no experience doing musicals with this age group.

Dr. Bobetsky's breadth and depth of experience in teaching music at all levels ensures the credibility and practicality of this book. *The Magic of Middle School Musicals: Inspire Your Students to Learn, Grow, and Succeed* will give you the tools you need to jump right in and do a musical with your students. The result will be a *musical* experience that you, your students, their parents, the school, and the community will fondly remember long after the curtain closes.

Russell L. Robinson, PhD
Professor of Music
Area Head for Music Education
University of Florida

PREFACE

When you adapt the score of a musical to middle school students' needs and capabilities, you create the conditions for success. I can tell you from personal experience that your students will retain positive memories of participating in the school musical for years to come.

Recently, while I was riding the New York City subway, a woman I did not recognize asked me, "Did you teach music at Junior High School 51 in Brooklyn?" I responded that I had. She said, "I was in your chorus!" It had been more than fifteen years since I taught at Junior High School 51, and I didn't recognize the woman until she told me her name. I asked if she had been a chorus member the year we performed at City Hall. She said that she joined the chorus later. Attempting to pin down the exact year she was in chorus, I asked, "Which musical were you in?" Her face lit up and she responded, without any hesitation, "*Grease*." She added that being in chorus and performing in the musical were very important to her as a student. After we went our separate ways, I thought about how remarkable it was that a thirty-something professional, married with two children, was able to so vividly remember her experience as a middle school chorus member in that musical. There are many reasons why being part of a musical was such a meaningful experience for her.

Being involved in a school production will appeal to your students on musical, social, and emotional levels. They will succeed musically and enjoy the social benefits of working together toward a shared goal. The drama and story line of the musical will provide them with a healthy outlet for emotional expression. Like my former student, your students' positive experiences will last a lifetime! Plus, you will derive professional and musical satisfaction from exploring the creative opportunities involved in producing your show. All of these things contribute to what I like to call the magic of middle school musicals. I encourage you to consider producing a musical in your school.

WHO THIS BOOK IS FOR

Regardless of the subject you teach, I wrote this book for you as the director of a musical production in your school. Throughout the book, you'll see that I address both you and your colleagues in other teaching specialties.

But it's not an ideal world, and your school may not have a perfect mix of dance, art, and other teachers. Share this book with any colleagues involved with your production, and have them read the parts relating to their specialties.

Better yet, encourage them to get their own copies. No matter where or what your colleagues teach in the future, as long as music is available in your school, *any* teacher—English, visual art, dance, math, physical education, it doesn't matter—can use this book to create musical theatre.

ACKNOWLEDGMENTS

Salimah Adawiya
Paul Anish
Zoe Armiger
Maria C. Bobetsky
Barbara Bosch
Daniel Burwasser
Harold Cherry
Mariana Cintron
Mimi D'Aponte
Jana Feinman
Bert Fink
Tonia Jeffery
Kevin Kidney
Harold Lehmann

Liz LoParro
Randy Houston Mercer
Judith Stanley Moroney
Nancy Newman
Angie Peterson
Frances S. Ponick
Michael Presser
Christopher Reali
Nicole Shorr
Gwendolyn A. Simmons
Barry Simpson
Louisa Thompson
Wojciech Typrowicz

I would like to extend a special thank-you to my wife, Maria C. Bobetsky, for her patience, understanding, suggestions, and support during the creation of this book.

❶

SELECT YOUR SHOW

Summer is approaching, and you are already thinking about the next school year. After selecting repertoire for the December holiday concert, you begin thinking about the spring semester. Once classes resume in January, how will you recapture the high level of enthusiasm and motivation that will have made the holiday concert so successful? Involving students and colleagues in planning and producing a spring musical can turn the proverbial "winter slump" into a time of learning and excitement.

You and your middle school choral students can reap many benefits from studying and performing a musical. Your students can develop their vocal performance skills as they explore this important genre of American music. Outstanding chorus members will have opportunities to perform as soloists and to master dramatic roles. You can express yourself creatively by arranging the vocal material to accommodate your students' abilities and grow professionally by developing new skills in areas such as staging, lighting, and choreography.

Planning and producing a musical gives middle school students the experience of actively participating in a form of theatre. Although the National Standards for the Arts recommend that middle schools offer comprehensive programs in theatre, many middle schools still do not offer such programs. A 1997 report by the National Assessment of Educational Progress notes that the theatre experience many middle school students do receive consists mainly of "reading the texts of plays in literature classes and attending occasional school performances" (Askew, Persky, and Sandene, 1998, p. 46).

THINGS TO CONSIDER

There are three basic criteria to use when selecting a musical for middle school students. First, the music needs to be vocally doable in some form by adolescent singers. Second, the plot and characters should interest the students and engage their emotions and imaginations. Finally, the story and setting should have the potential to involve other subject areas in a meaningful way. We'll discuss the first two of these criteria now, and the third in chapter 2.

Musical material that is vocally doable for adolescent voices usually is interesting, energetic, easily remembered, and relatively compact in range and tessitura. Music that is more abstract or that contains unusual and difficult intervallic leaps should be avoided. For example, *The Light in the Piazza* has a wonderfully written score, but the harmonic relationships and intervallic contour of many of its melodies would be too challenging for middle school singers; the melodic material would be difficult to learn and remember. In general, musical writing that can offer middle school students reasonable opportunities to develop phrasing, expression, and good tone is well worth pursuing.

Whenever you are working with middle school voices, you will probably need to adapt and arrange a considerable amount of the vocal material. Chapter 3 will explore the arranging process in detail. Remember that you must obtain permission from the copyright holder in order to arrange vocal material in a musical, especially if you plan to copy and distribute the music to your students. This information is available from music industry organizations, often via the Internet (www.mpa.org, www.ascap.com, and www.bmi.com can help with initial searches). You might start with *United States Copyright Law: A Guide for Music Educators* found at www.menc.org/resources/view/united-states-copyright-law-a-guide-for-music-educators.

What sort of plot and characters might middle school students find interesting? I have found that students of this age appreciate story lines involving romance, adventure, humor, and exotic locales. For example, *South Pacific*, which contained all of these elements, was a great success. Student performers played the characters of Bloody Mary and Luther Billis with great relish. The students who played the romantic leads of Nellie and Emile and Cable and Liat communicated these two love stories in a wonderful way. I found that the musical *Damn Yankees* appealed to my students because it involved baseball. The students also experienced vicarious pleasure at the actors' depictions of the temptress, Lola, and of Mr. Applegate, the devil in disguise.

On the other hand, middle school students are less interested in topics and story lines that are more introspective and intellectual, contain less action, or appear too childish. For example, middle school students might perceive the story lines of *Sunday in the Park with George* or *Brigadoon* to be too intellectual and slow moving. Depending on the maturity level and attitudes of your students, a musical like *Annie* may be perceived as too childish because it involves young children.

It is also important to think carefully about whether or not the musical you have in mind is appropriate for your particular school and community. Consider the ethnicities and religions of the families that populate your school. Some material in older musicals, while a product of the time when the show was written, may be considered offensive to particular ethnic groups today. For example, the song "I'm an Indian Too," from the original version of *Annie Get Your Gun* pokes fun at the names of tribal chiefs and contains lyrics and characterizations that could be considered offensive to people of Native American ancestry. I would probably omit that song, especially in a school whose population included Native Americans.

In addition, there are certain musicals that may not be appropriate for middle school students anywhere. An example might be *Grease*, due to its rather salty libretto. However, the licenser for *Grease* also offers a "sanitized" libretto that is more suitable for adolescent performers.

PERMISSIONS AND RENTALS

Once you have selected your musical, get in touch with the appropriate licenser in order to obtain permission to use the script. Licensers charge a royalty fee and a rental fee. The royalty fee gives you the right to produce a musical protected by copyright. The rental fee is for renting scripts, vocal and instrumental parts, and piano-vocal scores. Older shows typically are not as expensive as newer shows. Some, such as Gilbert and Sullivan operettas, are public domain and do not require any royalties to produce or arrange. However, you would still need to rent the script, parts, and score in order to produce a public domain work. The major licensers include Samuel French, Inc., Music Theatre International, and the Rodgers and Hammerstein Theatre Library:

Samuel French, Inc.
samuelfrench.com
45 West 25th Street
New York, NY 10010
Phone: (212) 206-8990 or (212) 206-8125
Fax: (212) 206-1429
E-mail: samuelfrench@earthlink.net

Music Theatre International
www.MTIShows.com

421 West 54th Street
New York, NY 10019
Phone: (212) 541-4684
Fax: (212) 397-4864
E-mail: licensing@MTIShows.com

Rodgers and Hammerstein Theatre Library
www.rnh.com
229 West 28th Street; 11th Floor
New York, NY 10001
Phone: (800) 400-8160 or (212) 564-4000
Fax: (212) 268-1245
E-mail: theatre@rnh.com

Each of these companies will send you catalogs and order forms
upon request and can also provide perusal materials, including li-
bretti and a piano-vocal score. In addition, the licensers can help
you gain access to a demo tape or original cast recordings.

Samuel French, Inc. handles both plays and musicals. Request
their musical catalog, which includes *Grease*, *The Wiz*, *Beauty and
the Beast*, and *The Me Nobody Knows*. The catalog offers very
brief summaries of each musical and lists the standard rental package. Samuel French, Inc. also offers band arrangements to accompany Gilbert and Sullivan's *The Mikado*, *HMS Pinafore*, and *The
Pirates of Penzance*.

Music Theatre International's catalog of musicals includes *West
Side Story*, *Little Shop of Horrors*, *Seussical*, *Fame*, and *Damn
Yankees*. The catalog provides commentary on each show, listing
the required cast, musical numbers, and instrumentation. In addition, MTI offers a Broadway Junior series containing shortened
and edited versions of famous musicals designed to be performed
specifically by middle school students. Representative shows include *Willy Wonka Junior*, *Fiddler on the Roof Junior*, *Guys and
Dolls Junior*, and *Godspell Junior*.

The Rodgers and Hammerstein Theatre Library houses musicals by Rodgers and Hammerstein, Richard Rodgers, Rodgers and Hart, Kurt Weil, and Andrew Lloyd Webber. The catalog offers a brief summary of each show along with a list of the musical numbers. There is also a Getting to Know series, designed for ages fourteen and under, that contains simplified versions of *Cinderella*, *Oklahoma*, *Once upon a Mattress*, and *The King and I*.

A Word about Royalties

It is extremely important that all music teachers and schools follow the required procedures involving royalties. The *New York Times* recently related the story of a public school in New York City that did not apply to the licenser for permission to use the musical *Chicago*. The school's drama teacher maintained that he had never been told about the need to follow this procedure. The licenser threatened the school with heavy financial penalties if it went ahead with the performance. In this particular instance, four New York City Council members and the speaker of the city council visited the licensing agency and persuaded them to allow the production to go ahead as scheduled. The school, in turn, promised to follow the correct procedures in the future. The article reported that, in general, "If a group puts on a performance that violates this rule, it could be liable for hundreds of thousands of dollars in damages" (Robertson, 2006).

Challenges

In order to successfully plan and produce a middle school musical, you may need to overcome several significant challenges. The most basic of these challenges is finding adequate rehearsal and preparation time. You'll also have to have the knowledge and the confidence necessary to arrange some of the musical material for middle school singers. Finally, you'll need to involve other subject areas in this project so that the resulting unit of study will be an especially meaningful learning experience for a large portion of the school community. This book offers strategies and solutions to all of these challenges, drawing upon the experience of seasoned teachers who have successfully produced musicals at the middle school level.

2

CREATE A UNIT OF STUDY

The choral director needs to promote the idea of creating a unit of study related to the musical. Share your thoughts with your principal and secure your school administration's support for the idea.

Before speaking with your colleagues, you may want to identify several musicals you think would be doable. By listening to original cast recordings or viewing DVDs, many of which can be found in your local library, you can eliminate those musicals that may not be suitable. Your reasons for eliminating certain musicals may include voice parts that are beyond the ability of middle school students, cast sizes that are too large or too small, too many cumbersome scene changes, or inappropriate subject matter. You can then order piano/vocal scores of the musicals you think might be doable and, by studying those scores, narrow your choices even further.

Now you are ready to meet with your colleagues in instrumental music, visual art, dance, theatre arts, language arts, and social studies to get key teachers excited about this project. As a result of your research, you will be prepared to suggest and recommend possible musicals that you feel the students could handle vocally with some modification. The musical you finally decide on should, of course, contain elements that all of the teachers can connect to their curricula and goals.

Working with your colleagues, create a written proposal for this unit of study to show to your principal, listing possible objectives for the various subject areas. Some people may feel that creating objectives and evaluation tools for a middle school musical can make things too analytical and dry. In my experience, the process of designing a unit of study based on a musical is a great way to involve the maximum possible number of students and colleagues. A unit of study documents the academic rationale for spending time and money on the musical, while creating schoolwide excitement and a meaningful learning experience for everyone. The celebrated American educator John Dewey (1938) maintained that a student's experience is a vital and necessary component of his or her education. The unit of study you and your colleagues will have created based on learning and performing a musical reflects John Dewey's philosophy of learning by doing.

Let's go through the process of designing a unit of study based on Rodgers and Hammerstein's *The King and I*, involving the disciplines of vocal and instrumental music, visual arts, dance, theatre arts, language arts, and social studies. We will identify several important activities/objectives for each subject area, link them to the National Standards, and suggest ways to measure student achievement. *National Standards for Arts Education* (Consortium of National Arts Education Associations, 1994) lists and discusses the standards for music, visual arts, dance, and theatre. The standards for English Language Arts and Social Studies are listed and discussed, respectively, in *Standards for the English Language Arts* (National Council of Teachers of English, 1996) and *Expectations of Excellence: Curriculum Standards for Social Studies* (National Council for the Social Studies, 1994).

IDEAS FOR OBJECTIVES AND ASSESSMENT BY SUBJECT AREA

Vocal Music

The activities and objectives you list for vocal music should reflect the things you will emphasize in your choral rehearsals. For example, you will probably want your students to perform the songs from *The King and I* accurately with good posture and breath control while also observing the appropriate dynamic and tempo markings. I am going to link these activities to Content Standard #1 of the National Standards for Music Education (Singing, alone and with others, a varied repertoire of music). However, you could also link observing dynamics and tempo markings to Content Standard #5 (Reading and notating music). The objectives can be written as follows: "Students will perform selected songs from *The King and I* accurately with good posture and breath control" and "Students will perform selected songs from *The King and I* observing the appropriate dynamic and tempo markings." You can assess student achievement in these areas by evaluating individual and small-group performances in class.

Before teaching the vocal numbers, you may want to have students listen to a professional cast recording of the musical in class. You might ask them to listen specifically for things like the basic rhythm, meter, and mode (major or minor) of selected songs. This activity is best linked with Content Standard #6 (Listening to, analyzing, and describing music), and the objective can be written as follows: "Students will listen to a professional cast recording of *The King and I*, identifying the basic meter, rhythm, and mode of selected songs." You can assess student achievement by evaluating student responses during group listening and discussion.

Finally, you might want to give your students opportunities to listen to and critique their singing, focusing on specific criteria. Involve the students in selecting criteria that reflect what you have emphasized in your rehearsals. For example, we talked earlier about singing accurately with good posture and breath control as well as observing appropriate dynamic and tempo markings. Any or all of these would be valid criteria. This activity falls under Content Standard #7 (Evaluating music and music performances), and the objective can be written as follows: "Students will listen to and critique their recorded performance using teacher- and student-developed criteria." You can assess student achievement by evaluating students' verbal or written critiques.

Instrumental Music

The activities and objectives you list should reflect the things you will emphasize in your band or orchestra rehearsals. For example, you will probably want your students to perform selections from the score to *The King and I* accurately and independently with good posture, playing position, and technique, while also observing the appropriate articulation, dynamic, and tempo markings. I am going to link these activities to Content Standard #2 of the National Standards for Music Education (Performing on instruments, alone and with others, a varied repertoire of music). However, you could also link observing articulation, dynamic, and tempo markings to Content Standard #5 (Reading and notating music). You can write the objectives as follows: "Students will perform selections from the score to *The King and I* as part of an ensemble, accurately and independently, with good posture, good playing position, and good breath, bow, or stick control" and "Students will perform selections from *The King and I* observing the appropriate articulation, dynamic, and tempo markings." You can assess student achievement in these areas by evaluating individual and small-group performances in class.

As suggested earlier for vocal music, have your instrumental music students listen to a professional cast recording of the musical in class before teaching the music. Ask them to listen specifically for things like the basic rhythm, meter, and mode (major or minor) of selected songs. This activity is best linked with Content Standard #6 (Listening to, analyzing, and describing music) and the objective can be written as follows: "Students will listen to a professional cast recording of *The King and I*, identifying the basic meter, rhythm, and mode of the selections they are learning." You can assess student achievement by evaluating student responses during group listening and discussion.

Finally, you might want to give your students opportunities to listen to and critique their playing, focusing on specific criteria. Involve the students in selecting criteria that reflect what you have emphasized in your rehearsals. For example, we talked earlier about playing accurately and independently with good posture, playing position, and technique, while also observing the appropriate articulation, dynamic, and tempo markings. Any or all of these would be valid criteria. This activity falls under Content Standard #7 (Evaluating music and music performances), and the objective can be written as follows: "Students will listen to and critique their recorded performance using teacher- and student-developed criteria." You can assess student achievement by evaluating students' verbal or written critiques.

Visual Art

The National Standards for Visual Arts require students to create art, select appropriate media for their work (including painting, drawing, and sculpture), and participate in the process of critiquing their own work and that of their peers. Middle school art students can work toward these goals as part of our unit of study. For example, they can create imaginative scenery and stage sets that enhance the production of a musical. These activities are related to Content Standard #1 of the National Standards for Visual Arts (Understanding and applying media, techniques, and processes) and the objective can be written as follows: "Students will create scenery and stage sets, working with paint, paper, and fabrics." You can assess student achievement in these areas by observing and evaluating each student's work in terms of both process and product.

In order for the scenery and sets to truly enhance the production, students need to select subjects that reflect the theme of the show. In the case of *The King and I*, the theme would be Southeast Asian history and culture. This activity is best linked with Content Standard #3 (Choosing and evaluating a range of subject matter, symbols, and ideas), and the objective can be written as follows: "Students will select subjects for the scenery that reflect the theme of Southeast Asian history and culture." You can assess student achievement by evaluating the selected subjects for relevance to the project's theme. Students can be asked to explain their choices of subject in a brief written statement.

The art teacher should provide students with structured opportunities to reflect on and critique their own work and the work of their peers. This activity falls under Content Standard #5 (Reflecting upon and assessing the characteristics and merits of their work and the work of others), and the objective can be written as follows: "Students will critique their own work and the work of their peers verbally and in writing, using teacher- and student-developed criteria." You can assess student achievement by observing students during class discussions and group critiques and by evaluating students' written responses.

Dance

You will probably want your student dancers to create some of the choreography. One way to do this is to use improvisation to generate movement for the choreography. This can be linked to Content Standard #2 of the National Standards for Dance (Understanding choreographic principles, processes, and structures), and the objective can be written as follows: "Students will use improvisation to generate movement for choreography." You can assess student achievement by observing each student's degree of participation in the improvisation exercises.

Once the choreography has been created, the students have to learn how to remember it and how to perform the movement sequences to music. These activities can be linked to Content Standard #1 (Identifying and demonstrating movement elements and skills in performing dance), and the objective can be written as follows: "Students will demonstrate the ability to remember and perform extended movement sequences to music." For assessment, the teachers and students can evaluate videotapes of rehearsals at successive intervals during the semester.

You will want your student dancers to develop and display a sense of rhythmic awareness and sensitivity. This can also be linked to Content Standard #1, and the objective can be written as follows: "Students will demonstrate rhythmic acuity." You can assess student achievement by observing and evaluating students' rhythmic acuity during the progress of the semester.

Your school may already have an established dance program. If not, you might have to recruit students who are interested in dancing in the musical. In either case, the basic objectives and activities you'll need to follow will remain the same.

Theatre Arts

Most of the work that theatre arts teachers will do with their students as part of the unit of study can be linked to Content Standard #2 of the National Standards for Theatre Arts (Acting by developing basic acting skills to portray characters who interact in improvised and scripted scenes). For example, students should become familiar with each character in the musical. They can demonstrate an understanding of the characters by creating short performances where the characters respond to imaginary situations and by reflecting on those performances in writing. These activities reflect Content Standard #2, and the objective can be written as follows: "Students will analyze the plot of *The King and I* in order to explain the motivation behind the characters' actions and invent character behaviors, communicating their findings through performance exercises and written reflections." You can

assess student achievement by monitoring the student performances and written reflections.

In order to present an effective production, theatre arts teachers
will need to help students develop good acting skills including eye
contact, concentration, vocal projection, and diction. A high level
of concentration can help student actors focus their mental and
physical energies on the performance, ignoring distractions such
as audience members walking in late, offstage noises, and crying
babies. Actors need to refine their diction and project their voices
so that audience members can hear and understand them. These
items are also related to Content Standard #2, and the objective
can be written as follows: "Students will demonstrate acting skills
including eye contact, concentration, vocal projection, and diction." You can assess student achievement by observing and evaluating individual students' initial skill level and subsequent growth.

Young actors also need to learn how to work well together in
small groups. Teachers can assign the rehearsal of specific scenes
to small groups of students, giving individual students responsibility for directing the rehearsals. These activities can be linked to
Content Standard #4 (Directing by organizing rehearsals for improvised and scripted scenes), and the objective can be written as
follows: "Students will work in small groups to rehearse scripted
scenes, demonstrating social, group, and consensus skills." You can
assess student achievement by observing how the students work
together and by evaluating their performance.

Language Arts

The libretto of *The King and I*, written by Oscar Hammerstein,
was influenced and inspired by Margaret Mortensen Landon's
book, *Anna and the King of Siam*. Landon's book, in turn, was
based on Anna H. Leonowens's memoir, *The English Governess at
the Siamese Court*. This memoir was written in 1870 and, although
it had been reprinted in the early twentieth century, many public

libraries will not have copies. However, students in language arts classes can read and use the libretto of *The King and I* and Landon's book, both of which are more readily available, to develop their reading, writing, and research skills.

For example, students can observe how the same topic and story are presented using the different genres of a libretto and a book. This activity can be linked to Language Arts Content Standard #2 (Students read a wide range of literature from many periods in many genres to build an understanding of the many dimensions, e.g., philosophical, ethical, aesthetic, of human experience), and the objective can be written as follows: "Through written essays, students will compare and contrast the libretto of *The King and I* with the book that inspired it, *Anna and the King of Siam*. They will explain how using different literary genres (libretto and memoir) can affect the presentation of a story." You can assess student achievement by evaluating the essays.

As they read and study the libretto and the book, students can also observe and describe how the characters' behavior and beliefs represent a contrast between the colonial British and Siamese cultures. For example, the Siamese were surprised that Anna wanted to work for a living. As Anna noted, the Siamese women in the king's harem considered themselves fortunate to live a life of leisure. This activity can be linked to Content Standard #1 (Students read a wide range of print and nonprint texts to build an understanding of texts, of themselves, and of the cultures of the United States and the world), and the objective can be written as follows: "Students will read and discuss the libretto of *The King and I* and the book *Anna and the King of Siam*. They will locate examples of Siamese attitudes toward women and Anna's attitudes toward the women of the king's harem as expressed in these two literary works." You can assess student achievement by evaluating student responses during class discussion.

Finally, students can locate past performance reviews of *The King and I*, read them, and then bring copies of these reviews to class. This can be linked to Content Standard #8 (Students use a variety of technological and information resources to gather and synthesize information and to create and communicate knowledge), and the objective can be written as follows: "Students will locate past performance reviews of *The King and I* using The *New York Times* Index and other databases recommended by the teacher and will read and bring copies of these reviews to class." For assessment, you can collect the printed reviews and verify that the reviews came from the recommended sources. In addition, you can have the students complete a worksheet requiring them to analyze the content and meaning of the reviews.

Social Studies

Students in social studies classes can develop a basic understanding of the geography, history, and culture of Thailand. For example, with respect to geography, they can learn to locate Thailand on a world map and to locate and identify neighboring countries such as Vietnam. These activities are related to Social Studies Content Standard # 3 (Study of people, places, and environments), and the objective can be written as follows: "Students will demonstrate the ability to locate Thailand on a world map and to locate and identify neighboring countries such as Vietnam." You can evaluate student success through observation and can ask additional questions to see whether students can explain Thailand's location relative to other countries and continents.

Students can also learn about the history and culture of Thailand and demonstrate their knowledge through class discussion and written essays. This can be linked to Content Standards #1 (Study of culture and cultural diversity) and #2 (Time, continuity, and change), and the objective can be written as follows: "Through participation in group oral presentations and written essays, students will demonstrate a basic knowledge of the history and culture of Thailand." You can assess student achievement by evaluating group presentations and essays.

Students can also compare selected elements of British colonial culture with those of the people of Southeast Asia. This activity can be linked to Content Standard #1 (Study of culture and cultural diversity), and the objective can be written as follows: "Students will develop questions designed to compare and contrast selected elements of British colonial culture, customs, and attitudes with those of the people of Southeast Asia." For example, students' questions might explore differences in religion, entertainment, or clothing. You can assess student achievement by evaluating students' written questions.

ADAPT THIS APPROACH FOR OTHER MUSICALS

You can successfully create units of study for many other musicals using this same approach. For example, while learning about and performing *Fiddler on the Roof*, students might examine how poor people lived in Russia at the time, describe the prevalent social order, conduct research on immigration and Jewish culture, discuss specific characteristics of Russian and Jewish folk art, as well as learn and perform traditional Russian and Jewish folk songs and dances.

How can such a unit of study be evaluated? First, I would recommend that each student be required to keep some type of ongoing journal throughout the entire duration of the project. Teachers should check the journals periodically to make sure that students do not fall behind. Toward the conclusion of the unit of study, students should use the material in their journals to create a reaction paper, which should form a portion of every student's grade. Next, I would recommend that the teachers go back to the original objectives and devise ways to specifically measure whether or not the students have achieved those objectives. Chapter 11 will discuss assessment procedures in greater detail.

Designing a successful unit of study related to a specific musical is hard work and requires collaboration among colleagues and the support of the school's administration. Once the unit of study has been developed, however, everyone involved will benefit from the clear learning objectives and sharp focus that a planned unit of study will provide.

3

ARRANGE THE MUSIC FOR
MIDDLE SCHOOL VOICES

Now that you have selected a musical, designed a unit of study related to that musical, and obtained the necessary permission from the rights holder, it is time to begin arranging the vocal material for your students. This chapter will focus specifically on suggestions and strategies designed to creatively address the vocal limitations of middle school singers within the context of studying and performing a musical.

DETERMINE YOUR SINGERS' VOCAL CAPABILITIES

First, consider the different vocal ranges of the students in your chorus. If you have a large number of girls in your group, their voices will most likely fall within one general range. Girls' singing voices at this age don't usually have distinct divisions (e.g., soprano and alto). Many of your boys' voices are no doubt changing. These boys may only be able to sing comfortably in a very limited range.

This chapter is a revision of Victor V. Bobetsky, "Arranging Musicals for Middle School Voices," reprinted from *Teaching Music*, February 2005. Copyright © 2005 by MENC: The National Association for Music Education. Used with permission.

There may be other boys in your chorus whose voices have already changed and who can sing the equivalent of a modified baritone part. Because of all these variables, it is safe to say that every middle school chorus is unique. The composition of your group will influence the strategies and methods you use when arranging music for your singers.

ADAPT A GIVEN MELODY TO THE SPECIFIC RANGE LIMITATIONS OF YOUR SINGERS

The following example is taken from a traditional Neapolitan folk melody that I arranged for seventh-grade chorus ("Tarantella," Boosey & Hawkes, 1992). Although this arrangement is not from a musical, I believe that it can illustrate the arranging process. Figure 3.1 shows the vocal ranges of the students. Figure 3.2 shows measures 1–8 of the original melody. Figure 3.3 shows the same measures, arranged in two parts.

In this two-part arrangement, the girls sing the original melody

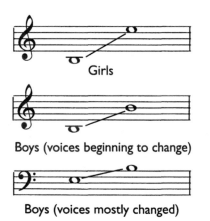

Girls

Boys (voices beginning to change)

Boys (voices mostly changed)

Figure 3.1.   Vocal Ranges of the Students for "Tarantella"

Figure 3.2. Measures 1–8 of "Tarantella" Melody

Source: "Tarantella" by Victor Bobetsky © copyright 1992 by Boosey & Hawkes, Inc. Reprinted by permission of Boosey & Hawkes, Inc.

(Part 1), which has a vocal range from the B a half-step below middle C to soprano E. All the girls should be able to sing in this range. The boys sing Part 2, which begins with a pedal-point ostinato on B. This note can be sung comfortably by boys with changing and changed voices. The rhythmically active repetition of the B (a note that the boys can sing well) will give these boys a sense of energy and confidence. Beginning at the fifth measure, boys with changing voices can sing Part 2 as written, while boys with changed

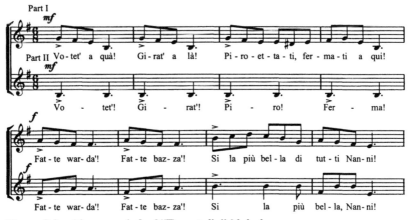

Figure 3.3. Measures 1–8 of "Tarantella" Melody

Source: "Tarantella" by Victor Bobetsky © copyright 1992 by Boosey & Hawkes, Inc. Reprinted by permission of Boosey & Hawkes, Inc.

voices can sing the same part an octave lower. The part writing is designed to create a boys' part with its own independent character rather than merely a harmonic accompaniment for the melody.

CREATE INTERESTING VOCAL PARTS

Whenever possible, write vocal parts that are interesting and fun to sing. Middle school students enjoy parts that have unique rhythmic and melodic characteristics. I arranged the song "I Gotta Keep Movin'" from the musical *Don't Bother Me, I Can't Cope* (Micki Grant, Fiddleback Music Publishing, 1973) for a seventh- and eighth-grade chorus with some boys in the beginning stages of vocal change as well as other boys who were approaching a baritone range. Figure 3.4 shows the vocal ranges of the students. Figure 3.5 shows the original melody (measures 4–12). Figure 3.6 shows an arrangement of these measures, written to accommodate this group of middle school singers.

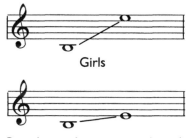

Girls

Boys (voices beginning to change)

Boys (voices mostly changed)

Figure 3.4. Vocal ranges of the students for "I Gotta Keep Movin'"

Figure 3.5. Measures 4–12 of "I Gotta Keep Movin'"

Source: "I Gotta Keep Movin'" from Micki Grant, *Don't Bother Me, I Can't Cope.* © 1972 Fiddleback Music Publishing Co., Inc. All rights administered by Warner-Tamerlane Publishing Corp. All rights reserved. Reprinted by permission of Warner Bros. Publications.

Figure 3.6. Measures 4–12 of "I Gotta Keep Movin'"

Source: "I Gotta Keep Movin'" from Micki Grant, *Don't Bother Me, I Can't Cope.* © 1972 Fiddleback Music Publishing Co., Inc. All rights administered by Warner-Tamerlane Publishing Corp. All rights reserved. Reprinted by permission of Warner Bros. Publications.

In this two-part arrangement, the girls sing the original melody (Part 1), which, again, has a vocal range extending from the B a half step below middle C to a soprano E. As in "Tarantella," all of the girls should be able to sing this part comfortably. The ostinato figure in Part 2 works well for boys whose vocal range is still limited, as well as for those boys with more developed voices. Notice how that ostinato line is derived from and echoes the rhythm of the last two notes of Part 1. This creates a rhythmically interesting dialogue between the two parts and helps to give Part 2 its own unique character. The first group of boys can sing Part 2 as written, and the second group of boys can sing the part an octave lower. Once again, the part writing is designed to create an independent, relatively easy part for the boys that they will enjoy singing.

Within the different arrangements you create, try to give each voice part an opportunity to sing some of the melody. A good illustration of this technique can be seen in the spiritual "Joshua Fit the Battle of Jericho," arranged in two parts by Jean Martin (Pro Art Publications, 1960). Figure 3.7 includes measures 3–6, where Part 2 initially has the melody. Figure 3.8 shows that, in measures

Figure 3.7. Measures 1–6 of "Joshua Fit the Battle of Jericho"

Figure 3.8.   Measures 10–15 of "Joshua Fit the Battle of Jericho"

Source: "Joshua Fit the Battle of Jericho," by Jean Martin. © 1960 (renewed) Belwin-Mills Inc. All rights reserved. Used by permission. Warner Bros. Publications.

10–15, Part 1 has the melody while Part 2 has a rhythmically and melodically independent ostinato.

Avoid writing too frequently in a block chord style (chorale-like) for this age group. One reason is that most middle school singers find it easier to sing in parts when each part has some degree of rhythmic or melodic independence. In addition, middle school students tend to feel that their own voice part is important when it has its own unique character and is not merely filling in a chord. Creating interesting and independent vocal parts will help to make your arrangements more musically interesting as well as more enjoyable for your middle school singers.

INCORPORATE CHORAL PARTICIPATION INTO SOLO NUMBERS

The vocal ranges of songs customarily performed as solos may exceed the ranges of individual middle school students, especially the boys. Consider arranging these numbers so that the appropriate character in the musical begins the solo alone but is joined by the chorus later in the song. The chorus can then either support the soloist or can replace the soloist as the song continues. This approach can heighten the dramatic effect of the song because everyone onstage is actively involved.

WHERE TO FIND ARRANGEMENTS FOR MIDDLE SCHOOL VOICES

Publishers

Cambiata Press (Don Collins, editor) is a publishing house that specializes in choral music designed to accommodate changing voices. www.cambiatapress.com.

Boosey & Hawkes's Building Bridges series (part of *The Choral Music Experience* and edited by Doreen Rao) focuses on choral literature for middle school, junior high, and beginning-level high school choruses. www.boosey.com.

Hal Leonard's Broadway Junior Collection is a series of fully authorized, abridged musicals arranged for children ages eight to fourteen. www.halleonard.com.

Arrangements

The following are a few representative samples of arrangements for middle school voices, spanning the years 1986 through the present, that work well for me now and have done so in the past:

Russell Robinson, "This Train," Heritage Music Press (Lorenz), 2007

Part 2 of this three-part arrangement of a traditional spiritual is written in a good range for middle school boys whose voices are changing.

Victor Bobetsky, "Limba, Limba Sally," Cambiata Press, 2004
This arrangement of a traditional Guyanese folk song is fun to sing. All three voice parts are rhythmic and lively. Boys with changing voices will be able to sing their part very comfortably.

Victor Bobetsky, "Tarantella," Boosey & Hawkes, 1992
This Neapolitan folk song, arranged for two parts, is part of Doreen Rao's Building Bridges series for developing voices. When used by a younger middle school or upper elementary chorus, Part 1 would be suitable for the girls and Part 2 for boys whose voices are changing. Boys with more developed voices can also sing Part 2 if they perform certain unison sections an octave lower than written.

Henry Leck, "South African Suite," Plymouth Music, 1991
This collection of three South African songs is arranged for three- and four-part treble voices. Part 4 would suit young boys whose voices are starting to change.

Andrea Klouse, "The E-ri-e Is A-risin'," Hal Leonard, 1986
This traditional folk song is arranged for two-part chorus. Part 2, which contains the melody line and some imitative entrances, can be effectively sung by boys with changing voices in a sixth- or seventh-grade chorus.

J. Springfield, "Fum, Fum, Fum," Cambiata Press, 1986
This well-known Spanish carol is arranged for three- or four-part variable voicing. Part 3 could be used for boys with changing voices. Part 4 is good for boys whose voices have changed. The arrangement is constructed so that Part 4 may be eliminated if the group has no changed voices.

AUDITIONING AND
CASTING PROCEDURES

Treat the audition and casting process professionally but gently. Remember that behind even the brashest facade, most middle school students have fragile egos and a tenuous sense of self-confidence.

PUBLICIZING THE AUDITIONS

Auditions should be open to all interested students. Publicize the date, time, location, and requirements for auditions well in advance. You can arrange to have this information announced in homerooms, in flyers posted around the school, and in a letter you send home to parents (in this book whenever we refer to parents, we mean parents, guardians, or anyone responsible for a child's welfare). Your letter could explain the time commitment involved in being part of the show and list the dates, times, locations, and requirements of the auditions. As part of this letter, ask parents to sign and return a tear-off form, giving their children permission to audition for a role.

Having these signed forms on hand in advance can help you avoid potential problems. For example, a student could audition for and receive an important role, but the parents, for any number of reasons, might not want their child to perform in the show. This would create an uncomfortable situation for the child, the parents, and the teacher. Some parents may feel the time commitment involved would interfere with the child's studies. In other cases, parents may have a religious objection to their child performing onstage in general or to some specific content in the show itself. You can save everyone a lot of aggravation and embarrassment by having parents indicate ahead of time whether or not their child has permission to audition for a role.

Work with your building administrator or office staff to schedule auditions for days and times that do not conflict with other school-related activities. In addition, you will want to be sure to decide on audition times that can accommodate students who go home by bus as well as those who walk home or are driven by their parents. If you do not follow these procedures, some students and their parents may claim that they were excluded from the audition process. Once you include every interested student in the audition process, you may discover talented students that you were not even aware of. One of these students may be just perfect for a particular role!

AUDITION PROCEDURES

Including other teachers in the audition process gives greater legitimacy to the audition results. It also allows any colleagues who may be working with you on acting, directing, and choreography to help you evaluate students' potential from another perspective. When choosing lead characters, you will want to see if the students can project their speaking voices, display confidence onstage, and demonstrate the necessary singing ability for the role.

For the first two criteria, have your students perform a prepared monologue. The passage can come from selected portions of the show's script that you distribute and assign in advance, or the students can choose their own material (not necessarily related to the show). The first approach is more specific because it allows you to focus on how the students deliver some of the actual lines their characters will need to speak in the show. The second approach is more holistic. When a student delivers a passage he or she has chosen and presumably is motivated to perform, you should be able to get a true sense of that student's potential as an actor.

Music teachers use a variety of materials for auditions. Some teachers allow the students to choose and perform any song they know and love. Others assign the same selection to everyone trying out for a particular part. This selection is often a song that the character sings in the show. If you do the latter, make sure to distribute and go over the music with your students at least several weeks prior to auditions.

For lead parts that involve solo singing, you'll need to get a clear sense of each student's range and tessitura (the portion of the range that is most comfortable for the student to sing in). This can be done by administering a simple voice test. Have plenty of blank index cards available and make a card for each auditioning student. Notate what appear to be the highest and lowest notes in each student's vocal range as well as the student's tessitura. You should also write down any quick impressions you have of each student's voice. It is easy to forget details after auditioning many students, so a written record of your impressions is necessary in order to help you make and to justify your casting decisions. For example, you might make a written notation on a student's index card that a student has a breathy vocal quality or has difficulty projecting his/her voice. Similarly, make note of any outstanding qualities you notice in a student's audition, such as a clear, pure singing tone or excellent diction.

After auditioning everyone who is interested in the lead roles, you and your colleagues will be able to decide on a short list of applicants. Call back this group of finalists and have them repeat their performances. You should now be able to choose the leading members of your cast.

Now it is time to fill the minor speaking roles. As you conducted the auditions for lead roles, you may have noticed certain students whose personalities, mannerisms, or physical qualities seemed well suited to one of these smaller parts. If such a student was not selected for a lead role, cast him or her in the smaller part. In addition, there may be a student whose abilities are limited but who really wants to be in the cast. One teacher told me about a talented boy with a developmental/physical problem that caused him difficulty figuring out spatial relationships. The boy wanted badly to be in the show and the teacher felt that it was important to include the boy in the production. The teacher cast him in a speaking role alongside a strong girl who helped him function well.

NOTIFY STUDENTS AND PARENTS OF AUDITION RESULTS

As soon as auditions are over and the parts have been assigned, send out a letter to selected students and their parents, congratulating the students on the role they have received. Tell the students that although they may not have received the part they wanted, they are now members of a wonderful cast. You can attach a tear-off form to this letter stating: "My son/daughter accepts this role in the musical and understands the responsibilities of attending all rehearsals and performances." Ask the parents to sign and return this form to you. Figure 4.1 contains a sample letter and form that you can use. The tear-off form in this sample letter has a space where parents can volunteer their services to help with ticket sales, costumes, publicity, and other activities. We'll talk more about this in chapter 9.

Some students who did not receive the role they wanted will be very upset. They may feel inadequate and humiliated and will ei-

Name and Address of Your School

Dear [Name of Student] and Parents:

Congratulations! You have been chosen for the part of _____ in our musical production. You may not have gotten the part you really wanted, but you are still a member of a wonderful cast. The audition process is always a difficult one for the student as well as for the director. It is, however, an important process that builds character and prepares you for your High School Experiences. Self-confidence and believing in yourself are important areas of growth to nurture.

Our rehearsals will begin immediately with learning the music. Beginning in [month] we will rehearse on [specify days of the week] from [starting to ending times]. Please remember that as we draw closer to our production date we may have to extend the rehearsal times.

Thanks to you and your parents for your patience and understanding during auditions—a difficult time in our production. Let's really support the show.

Finally, we could use help in the area of costumes, scenery, props, ticket sales, etc. . . . Any offers of assistance will be very much appreciated.

Please feel free to call me with any questions or concerns at [phone number].

Sincerely,

Name of Director

* *

Kindly detach and return to [Name of Director] immediately.

My son/daughter accepts his/her role in the musical and understands the responsibilities of attending all rehearsals and performances.

Student Name (Print)	Parent Signature and Phone Number

For Parents Only:

I am interested in helping with the musical in the following areas:

_____ Costumes   _____ Ticket Sales   _____ Backstage Supervision

_____ Help in painting scenery, building props, and set design

_____ Publicity   _____ Cast Party

Figure 4.1.   Letter Notifying Students and Parents of Audition Results

ther communicate this to you verbally, act out their frustration in class, or withdraw through sulking behavior. You will need to be especially patient with these students. Make time to speak with each of them individually. Explain that just because they were not chosen for a particular role doesn't mean that they have no ability. It just means that their abilities are suited to something different. You might even describe the positive attributes they demonstrated at the audition that caused you to select them for the role they actually received. These kinds of conversations will usually resolve the problem.

DOUBLE CASTING

Assigning understudies to the lead parts, which is common in professional theatre, would not be appropriate in middle school since understudies might never get the chance to perform the role onstage. However, if you have many enthusiastic and capable students, you may want to consider double casting. Double casting means that you will select two separate lead casts for your production. For double casting to work, you will need to schedule more than one performance. For example, have one group of actors perform the lead roles the first night and a second group the next night. While double casting is not normally used in professional theatre, it makes sense in a middle school production since it offers as many students as possible the opportunity to perform. Also, should one of your lead actors have an emergency one night and be unable to perform, the actor playing the same part in the other cast would be prepared to step in.

NONTRADITIONAL CASTING

Traditional casting places emphasis on whether the actors display the physical or ethnic characteristics usually attributed to a role.

Over the past several decades, it has become acceptable to use nontraditional casting in professional, amateur, and school productions. Nontraditional casting is an approach to casting that is not restricted to choosing actors that "look the part." In the world of professional theatre, the concept of nontraditional casting has been cited in efforts to open more roles to women and other underrepresented groups.

One Broadway production that used nontraditional casting to great acclaim is the 1994 Broadway revival of Rodgers and Hammerstein's *Carousel*, where Audra MacDonald, an African American actress, received a Tony award for her portrayal of the white, New England character of Carrie Pepperidge. Another production replete with nontraditional casting is ABC TV's 1997 remake of Rodgers and Hammerstein's musical, *Cinderella*. The African American actress, Brandy Norwood, played Cinderella; Bernadette Peters played the wicked stepmother; the Asian American actor Paolo Montalban played the prince; and Whoopi Goldberg and Victor Garber played the queen and king. You can read more about the history of nontraditional casting in musicals by consulting the journal *American Theatre*.

Opera companies employ an even more significant amount of nontraditional casting than theatre, since casting for an opera is so dependent on the singers' vocal quality and range. In professional and amateur opera companies it is commonplace to see older women cast as teenagers, dark-skinned singers cast as Northern Europeans, light-skinned singers cast as Egyptian princesses, and couples who, in the plot, would realistically be of the same ethnicity being portrayed by singers in multiple combinations of races and ethnicities.

The value of using a nontraditional casting approach in a school setting is that it gives you the flexibility to choose the best person for the role, whether they "look the part" or not. For example, in a school production of *Damn Yankees*, I cast a small-sized boy who was able to effectively demonstrate mischief and cunning as Mr.

Applegate (the Devil). While some could argue that this boy, who was shorter than everyone else in the cast, might not be perceived as very threatening, we based our decision on the student's unique and lively interpretation of the role. Our Mr. Applegate brought the house down!

You can also use a nontraditional casting approach when choosing actors for pairs and combinations of characters. When I directed a middle school production of *South Pacific*, I cast a gregarious student, who was willing to take direction and who happened to be dark skinned, as Bloody Mary. I selected for Liat, Mary's daughter, a girl who exhibited the sensitivity, gentleness, and subtle coquettishness that is the essence of Liat's character. Our choice for Liat happened to be a light-skinned Hispanic girl. In my opinion, the issue of whether or not our Liat looked as if she could really be Bloody Mary's daughter was irrelevant. It was far more important to find and cast the student actors who could best personify the spirit of each character.

A PLACE FOR EVERYONE

It is important for all middle school students to be able to participate in many different types of activities so they can discover what they like to do and learn where their talents and interests lie. The middle school musical allows students to explore what it is like to be part of a large theatrical production. Your responsibility is to select the best person for each part. However, once the auditions are over, make sure that every student who tried out for a role receives some kind of onstage part.

5

INVOLVE YOUR
PERFORMING GROUPS

Try to involve as many students and music teachers as possible in the show by including your school's performing groups. This will enhance the production and give everyone the opportunity to participate in the show's success. Most middle schools have some kind of choral program that meets as part of the school day or as an after-school activity. Many middle schools also have a band and perhaps a string orchestra. Additional performing groups might include guitar, recorder, or Orff ensembles. This chapter will help you decide if and how you can involve these students in the musical.

WORKING WITH THE CHORUS

If you are the chorus teacher, you can do a lot during regular chorus rehearsals to prepare for the show. In addition to teaching the music to the chorus, soloists, and ensembles, you can help interested students prepare for lead auditions, and get students involved in the story by having them participate in dramatic readings of portions of the libretto. All of your choral students will then be familiar with their music, the entire story line, the solo parts, and the actual libretto of the show well before combined rehearsals begin onstage.

The Glue that Holds the Show Together

The chorus was an extremely important component of the show in the middle school productions I directed. Students not only sang the choral parts but also supported various lead characters by singing along in sections of their solo numbers. The extent of the choral involvement in solo numbers depended on the vocal abilities of each lead character. If a lead character could carry an entire solo number well, then the chorus did not need to be involved in that song. In cases where a lead character could sing the first section of the number well but wasn't vocally strong enough or lacked a wide enough range or vocal power to complete it, the chorus would join in at a designated point.

Having the chorus enter mid-number is a strategy that can provide both support and dramatic emphasis. I used this approach for "Whatever Lola Wants, Lola Gets" in a production of *Damn Yankees*. Our Lola sang the first two long phrases of the song whenever they appeared (the most familiar part of the song), and the chorus echoed her during her rests. When the melody and harmony became more chromatic and the range more extensive ("I always get what I aim for . . ."), I had the chorus sing the melody with her.

In the rare cases where a lead character was chosen for his/her acting ability but did not have much vocal ability at all, I had the chorus sing the entire number while the actor was engaged in some related dramatic activity. For example, in a production of *South Pacific*, our Bloody Mary, a terrific actress, was not skilled enough vocally to sing "Bali Ha'i." We adapted to this situation by having the chorus sing "Bali Ha'i" while Bloody Mary performed expressive hand gestures, dividing her attention between the audience and the island portrayed on the stage backdrop. This presentation of "Bali Ha'i" was dramatically effective and suitably magical.

Prepare Students for Lead Auditions

Each January, I taught the chorus to sing several of the most important solo numbers of the show in unison. If you do this, make sure to create special ostinato lines or separate parts for those boys whose changing voices may not allow them to sing the melody as written (see chapter 3). As we practiced the songs, I gave any interested students opportunities to sing all or part of the song as a solo in class. This helped to build students' confidence and prepared them to audition vocally for the lead roles, should they want to. This system worked well because most of the students who tried out for singing roles were already chorus members. However, we also encouraged interested students who were not chorus members to audition. In order to give those students equal preparation, I offered them the option of attending chorus rehearsals to learn the songs. If attending chorus rehearsals was not feasible for them, I would arrange to meet with the students as a group at an alternate time in order to teach them the music they would need to audition.

Auditions for lead roles usually involve spoken dialogue in addition to singing. You can devote a small amount of time during each choral rehearsal to script reading and dramatization. Use selections of the script that lead up to a choral number you are rehearsing or that the chorus has already learned. Assign students parts in the script, have them perform the scene, and then segue into the choral number. This gives the students the experience of a mini-performance in the classroom.

Each time you rehearse the scene, arrange for different students to read from the script so that eventually, every interested student will have read every part. I found that this teaching strategy keeps the students excited about learning the script and the music, increases their understanding of the musical, and helps prepare students for auditions. In fact, even those students who have no desire to audition for a role and are happy just to be in the chorus tend to learn the script so well that I have often seen them mouthing every word as the actors speak during rehearsals. Clearly everyone's memory retention skills are being effectively sharpened by these activities!

YOUR INSTRUMENTAL ACCOMPANIMENT

The instrumental accompaniment you end up using will vary depending on the musical you are presenting and on the type and level of the instrumental ensembles in your school. A Rodgers and Hammerstein musical is generally scored for a twenty-piece orchestra including winds, strings, brass, and percussion. Rock musicals require fewer instruments and generally do not call for members of the string family. For example, the score of *Footloose* is written for keyboard, electric bass and guitar, drum set, horns, and a flute/tenor sax/clarinet part originally designed for one player. While many middle schools may not have all of these resources available, you can find creative solutions to achieve an effective accompaniment for any musical among the suggestions that follow.

Find Capable Pianists

First, you must find one or more good pianists who can handle the piano/vocal reduction of the score. Are there any student accompanists or other faculty members capable of doing this? If not, see if you can get competent pianists from an area high school, college, or community music school. Explain to your school administrator that the show's success depends on having capable pianists. Arrange to pay them through whatever funds the school or the PTA can make available.

It is always a good idea to involve more than one pianist. This will prevent any individual's rehearsal schedule from becoming too heavy. In addition, should one pianist have an emergency and not be able to attend a rehearsal or performance, there will always be a backup pianist available. If you are lucky enough to have more than one pianist, divide the rehearsal and performance time among them so that no one pianist becomes overburdened. I suggest assigning one pianist for each night of the show so that all pianists have an opportunity to play for at least one performance and receive their well-deserved recognition. If you only have one performance and two pianists, have one pianist perform for the first half of the show and the other for the second half. This way, no one will feel left out.

If you are a seasoned pianist and no other qualified person is available, consider accompanying the show yourself. One advantage of this arrangement is that you will now have the opportunity to directly produce at the piano the tempo, dynamics, and phrasing you envision. One significant disadvantage is that you will no longer be physically available to supervise any other aspects of the performance or to troubleshoot any problems that might arise. If you do accompany the musical yourself, make sure to clearly delegate all of your other responsibilities for the night of the performance to trusted colleagues well in advance.

Create a Small Ensemble

If your school does not have a band or orchestra, and you want the accompaniment to your musical to be more than piano alone, find talented students or colleagues who play bass and drums. You can effectively accompany any musical with a combination of piano, bass, and drums. The piano carries the melody, the bass adds depth to the sound, and the drumming provides rhythm, vitality, and color. This minimalist ensemble can give a greater rhythmic emphasis to the score than using piano alone, and hearing the rhythm clearly will help your students onstage. The drum is especially important if there will be dancing in the show. A drummer who is a good timekeeper will be of great help to the dancers.

Within this small ensemble, some variations are possible, depending on the talent available. The bass can be electric or string bass. If you can't find a bass player, find someone who can play an electric keyboard and have that person play the bass line with their left hand. Many scores to musicals have attractive flute, clarinet, or trumpet parts. If you have any of these instrumentalists available, add them to your small ensemble.

If these musicians are not available, but you still want to be able to hear the parts, consider using a synthesizer. If you can get access to a synthesizer with a full-sized keyboard (eighty-eight keys), and someone who can play it, you can easily add these parts to your accompaniment. Simply push the button for the instrumental sound you want and play the instrumental line on the keyboard. For example, in a production of *Joseph and the Amazing Technicolor Dreamcoat*, one music teacher successfully used an ensemble of string bass, drums, and piano, with the synthesizer playing some of the additional instrumental solos.

Feature Your Instrumental Performing Groups

If your school has a band or string program and the students are able to perform the score to the musical, have them do so. Try to schedule any other concert commitments for the semester early in the spring. Include a song or two from the show and information about the upcoming production, encouraging students and parents to attend. Once this concert is over, the students will be free to focus all of their attention on learning the score to the show. If the group is not able to handle the entire score, perhaps the instrumental teacher can create a simplified version of the score that the students can perform. If this is not feasible, consider having the students accompany specific musical numbers that they are able to play. Whatever else you do, maintain your minimalist ensemble of piano, bass, and drums as the core accompaniment for the show. This ensemble, especially the piano, can help keep things moving if the instrumentalists falter.

Adapting an Orchestral Score for Your Band

Suppose you are planning to present a musical whose score is written for orchestra, such as a Rodgers and Hammerstein show. If you have string players, use them. If you do not have string players, but have a band program, use the band. The band director can substitute "like" instruments (instruments that play in similar registers) to stand in for the string instruments you do not have.

For example, flutes can be easily substituted for first and second violins. If you have at least eight flutes, this should be feasible. You can divide them evenly or put five flutes on the first violin part and three on the second violin part. The flute players will be able to read the violin parts without any problem since both flutes and violins are C instruments. Your band director may need to simplify the parts a bit in order to accommodate students' needs and abilities. Some sections of the violin parts will need to be transposed an octave higher so the flutes can play in a more comfortable range and so their sound will project more. If you do not have enough flutes to cover both violin parts, you can assign the flutes you do have to the first part and have the clarinets play the second part. However, since the clarinet is a B-flat instrument and the violin is written in C, someone will need to transpose and rewrite the second violin part so the clarinet players can read it.

Another problem the band director will face is that orchestral scores may not contain parts for some traditional band instruments such as baritone horns and saxophones. However, there may be other parts in the score that these instruments can play. For example, the baritone horn can double on the bassoon part. Because these two "like" instruments are also both C instruments, the baritone horn players will be able to read the bassoon part easily. The baritone horn can also double on the cello part. However, since some of the notes in the cello's higher range are not playable on the baritone horn, the band director may need to do some rearranging of the part. If you have a lot of alto saxophones but no French horn, it might be a good idea to rewrite the French horn part for the alto saxophone players. These can be considered "like" instruments since they play in similar registers. Using the same approach, the band director can rewrite the baritone horn part for baritone saxophones.

Depending on the skill and imagination of your band director, he or she may perceive arranging and rewriting instrumental parts as either a creative activity or a chore. In any case, it can be time consuming. The alternative to doing the arranging and rewriting "in-house" is to try to find a band arrangement of the show's original score. For example, the Rodgers and Hammerstein Theatre Library (www.rnh.com) has developed a band arrangement for the score of *Oklahoma*. Unfortunately, there are not many such arrangements, and especially not for middle school–age band students. Music teachers interested in creating these types of arrangements might have a good chance of finding publishers.

Use Other School Ensembles as Part of the Accompaniment

Suppose your school does not have a string or a band program but does have a guitar ensemble. You may already be using piano, bass, and drums to accompany the show, but it would be nice to involve the guitar ensemble in some way. You could ask the guitar instructor to look over the score to the musical. Are there any solo numbers that could be effectively accompanied by the guitar ensemble? A wonderful example is the song "Edelweiss" from *The Sound of Music*, which Captain Von Trapp sings while playing the guitar. If your Captain Von Trapp does not play the guitar, have him hold the guitar and pretend to play, while the guitar ensemble accompanies him. When using a middle school guitar ensemble to accompany a song, make sure the song has relatively simple and slow-moving harmonies.

If your school has a recorder ensemble, see if there is a good place to feature these students in the show as well. You might use a recorder group to accompany the children who sing "Dites-Moi Pourquois" in *South Pacific*. Or perhaps your school has an Orff ensemble. If so, look for places in the show where this group might be appropriate and effective. It might be fun to use Orff instruments to accompany a song that is sung by children in a classroom or other instructional setting such as "Do Re Mi" from *The Sound of Music* or "Getting to Know You" from *The King and I*.

Volume, Balance, and Live Accompaniment

Whatever the nature or size of your accompanying ensemble, make sure that the group does not play too loudly. Explain to the students that there is a big difference between accompanying a song and accompanying a dance. The volume must come down for a song so that the instruments do not overpower the singers. The volume for a dance can and should be louder to highlight the rhythm and support the dancers.

I would never attempt to perform a musical without some form of live accompaniment. While it may be tempting to consider using prerecorded, taped, or computerized accompaniments, there are some significant disadvantages to this approach. Use of a prerecorded accompaniment can result in a rigid, metronomic performance and can limit your ability to provide creative leadership. You will be unable to quickly compensate if your singers' tempo tends to rush or drag at any point in the performance. Finally, the show can be ruined should you experience problems with the equipment and have no live musicians to take over in an emergency. Enjoy the excitement and artistic satisfaction of working with live music and live musicians!

6

ORGANIZATION, SCHEDULING, AND YOUR MASTER PLAN

As music director, and general coordinator of the production, it is in your interest to initiate a master plan in order to make sure everything goes as smoothly as possible and according to schedule.

PLAN AHEAD

Early in the fall semester is the time to develop a schedule and timeline to address all aspects of the spring production. Your master plan should clarify what needs to happen, when it needs to happen, and where it should happen. It will help to guide everyone from selecting the show before the summer, through January auditions, to opening night. The information in this chapter is based on the sample timeline found in table 6.1, which is meant to be a general guide. Although everyone's circumstances are different, it will always be a great help to put the tasks and activities that need to be completed in preparation for your production on paper. You can adapt the format of this sample guide to your needs by omitting entries that may not be relevant and/or adding other entries that are unique to your situation.

This chapter will suggest ways to plan for the optimal use of your school's available rehearsal and performance space, and will help you take control of the organizational maze of opening night activities prior to curtain time.

SOLICIT IDEAS FROM YOUR COLLEAGUES

Discuss the calendar timeline with your colleagues (especially the theatre arts, dance, and visual arts teachers). Ask for their suggestions about what times, dates, and rehearsal spaces would work best for them. Here are some additional items you should plan for:

How, when, and where you will schedule auditions.

Rehearsal times and locations for each group involved in the performance (main characters, chorus, dancers, band students, stage crew, tech crew, lighting crew)—highlight when each group will need to use the auditorium.

Uninterrupted time in the auditorium for the art teacher and students to create and design the scenery.

Times and locations for combined rehearsals, which will take place in the auditorium beginning two weeks prior to the performance, and dress rehearsals, which will take place one or two days before the performance.

Locations and room numbers that each group of students will report to on the night of the performance.

Let your colleagues know that you will take the lead in presenting the final version of the plan to your principal. Be sure that it reflects everyone's needs. You want to avoid last-minute crises and potential conflicts among teachers over rehearsal spaces and times.

A Word about the Auditorium

Most middle school productions are held in the auditorium. Remember that the school auditorium is used throughout the year for many different purposes, such as guest artist performances and school assemblies. Overcrowded schools sometimes use the auditorium for study halls, for detention, or even to hold combined classes on days when many teachers are absent. This is why it is critical that you reserve the auditorium in advance for the times when you know you will need it. If your school does not have an auditorium and you end up using an alternate space such as a large theatre room with a stage, the gym, or the cafeteria, you should apply and adapt the suggestions in this chapter to suit your particular needs.

MEET WITH YOUR PRINCIPAL

Schedule a time to discuss this plan with your principal and to ask for his/her support. Your conversation should take place during early fall, when the principal is likely to be planning the spring schedule. This way, your requests can be considered and approved well in advance. During this meeting, tell your principal what your colleagues need to do in the auditorium to prepare for the show, and when they will need access in order to do it.

The following are some points you may want to cover.

Choral and Theatre Arts Teachers

The choral and theatre arts teachers will need to start using the auditorium in mid-January, once casting is completed, to begin working onstage with the leading actors. In addition, as the semester goes on, these teachers will be working together on scenes that may involve the chorus and several of the actors. If the principal can give the choral and theatre arts teachers schedules containing a common preparation or free period, they can accomplish some of this work together during the school day.

Art Teacher

The art teacher will need access to the auditorium in mid-November in order to take measurements for the scenery. During the final month of rehearsals, the art teachers and students need to be given specific times when they can take over the auditorium to create and complete the scenery and stage sets.

Dance Teacher

The dance teacher will begin teaching students their parts sometime in January. If the school has a separate dance space, much of the initial work can be done there. However, if the only dance space available is the auditorium, time should be blocked out in the auditorium for dance rehearsals.

Choral and Instrumental Music Teachers

The choral and instrumental music programs usually have their own rehearsal rooms in the building. As long as this is the case, neither will need to use the auditorium as a full group until a minimum of three weeks before the performance. It is generally more difficult to run a choral, band, or orchestra rehearsal in the auditorium than in the regular rehearsal rooms, so there is no reason to do this any earlier than necessary.

Teachers should use the time spent in their own rehearsal rooms to work out all the musical kinks and details before the first rehearsal in the auditorium. That way, once in the auditorium, the choral director can focus on physically positioning the singers onstage and helping them learn to enter and exit the stage area gracefully. In addition, the choral director will want to hear how the group sounds onstage and make whatever changes in the sound that seem necessary. The instrumental music teacher can focus on refining the group's sound to suit the space and can help the students achieve the correct balance needed to accompany solo singers and the chorus.

THE NIGHT OF THE SHOW

There will be a whirlwind of activity in your school building on opening night prior to curtain time. Warm-up sessions for different groups of performers, sound and lighting checks, and a final check on props are just a few of these activities. It is critical that you make advance preparations to ensure that events leading up to curtain time flow as smoothly as possible.

Give Everyone Clear Instructions

Every student, teacher, and parent helper must be told in advance exactly what time to report to school as well as the specific location they are to report to (room number or backstage area). It is extremely important that all the people involved in the show report to school at least one hour before the curtain time and head to their assigned location. Here is a typical rundown of where you may want your various show members to report and what they should do once they get there:

Band members to the band room to tune and warm-up
Chorus members to the chorus room to warm-up
Stage crew to the backstage area to check that all large scenery items are where they need to be
Prop master to the stage area to double-check that all props are ready and in place
Lighting crew to the lighting booth to review cues and setups
Tech crew to the auditorium for sound checks
Stage manager to the auditorium to check on the progress of the prop manager and the stage and lighting crews

Dancers to the dance rehearsal space for their warm-up (If your school has no separate dance rehearsal space, the dancers could report to the auditorium for a brief warm-up on the stage or to the gym where it might be possible to do stretching exercises on mats.)

Parent or teacher volunteers staffing the warm-up rooms to those locations.

Make sure to notify everyone of these details in writing several weeks ahead of time. It is also helpful to send a letter to the parents or guardians of every student involved in the show. Your letter should include the dates and times of the dress rehearsal(s) and performance(s). Specify the exact time the children need to arrive at school and the room numbers they should report to on the night of the performance. Request that the parents meet their children in those rooms after the show. In addition, you may want to ask the parents to make sure their children eat a light dinner before they arrive at school. This can prevent students from feeling faint or dizzy during the performance. Include a tear-off form for the parents to sign and return indicating that they have read the letter and will ensure that their child arrives at his/her designated location on time.

Warm-Up Sessions

Once the students are assembled in their assigned locations, all performers should go through a fifteen-minute warm-up session.

Band/Orchestra After making sure that all the instruments have been well tuned, band or orchestra teachers should lead their students in warm-ups focusing on balance, blend, and articulation. You can accomplish all of these things by having the students play scales at a moderate pace and volume. Work on balancing the sections and blending the sound. Play the scales legato and staccato. Then, have the group practice the first few measures of some of the numbers in the show in order to remind everyone of the starting tempos and dynamic levels. If there is still time, have the students play one of the more difficult passages in the score slowly and relatively softly so that the students remain relaxed and their minds and ears can focus on the notes and the phrasing.

Chorus The choral teacher can start the warm-up session with body stretches. Have everyone stand and do shoulder rolls forward and backward for muscle relaxation. Then, work on breath control. Have the students exhale until they are out of breath. Then have them take in air slowly as if filling up a balloon and exhale gradually and silently to your count. Make sure their shoulders are relaxed. Have the students repeat the exercise, this time singing "ooh" on one unison pitch while they exhale. Spend a few minutes singing each pure vowel in unison on a five-note descending pattern beginning at a medium pitch level. Then, you can ask the students to harmonize in triads, moving up by half steps. Do all these things slowly and with a relaxing feel to it. Use the remaining few minutes of the warm-up to practice entrances to a few of the numbers to establish tempo and dynamic levels.

Theatre Arts Theatre arts teachers can begin their warm-up exercises with stretches and muscle-relaxing exercises similar to what the choral teachers do. They can then lead the students in a relaxed theatre game that emphasizes focus and communication. Try using the mirror game described in chapter 7. The students will be so busy concentrating and watching their partners' movements and expressions that they will forget about being nervous.

Dance One idea for beginning opening night warm-up exercises is to lead the students in some yoga-like stretches. Then, move to exercises that encourage students to sharpen their focus. For example, ask them to imagine a phrase and to feel the amount of time it will take to perform the phrase. Then have them move to the phrase, filling the room with their movement, as if their arms could reach to the walls and their heads to the ceiling. Or, you can do some group exercises where students "pass around" a movement phrase. For example, one student performs an original phrase. As the phrase draws to a close, the dancer moves or gestures toward another student who becomes the receiving student. The receiving student can repeat the same phrase or create a new phrase. In either case, he or she will perform the phrase, and "pass it on" to another student in the same manner. Continue this exercise until everyone has had a turn.

Holding Pen

At the conclusion of the warm-up exercises, encourage the students to relax until it is time to go onstage. However, it is always a challenge to get students to relax when they are about to perform. They will be full of energy and excitement. It helps if you tell the students in advance to bring something to read or a puzzle to work on. Some schools arrange to have VCRs sent to these "holding rooms" so that the students can watch a movie. Activities such as these should help the students to calm down and conserve their energies for the performance. Here are some things to remember as you plan for your time in the "holding pen":

- Have water available, whether it is from school drinking fountains or bottles of water that you can store in the room.
- Speak to the custodians in advance to make sure the student bathrooms will be open and well stocked.
- Make sure that the ventilation in your auditorium and in your rehearsal rooms is working properly. Open the windows enough to let in some fresh air. An auditorium or rehearsal room in which the air is overheated, stuffy, or stale can affect the choral sound and may also contribute to some students becoming ill and/or fainting.

Move from the Holding Rooms to the Auditorium

Create a system designed to notify teachers assigned to holding rooms about ten minutes before their group needs to enter the stage area. Some schools use student runners, supervised by a teacher or an assistant principal, for this purpose. This gives the teacher in charge time to help the students regain focus and assume their assigned lineup positions.

Have the parent or colleague who is helping out in your room make sure the students leave their personal belongings behind. Once everyone has exited the room, this helper should make sure all doors leading to the room are locked.

Proceed quickly and quietly to the stage entrance.

ASSEMBLE YOUR TEAM

There is an incredible amount of detail and last-minute checking that must be done during the hour or so before curtain time. Arrange for a team including your stage manager, selected parents, teachers, and administrators to function as your eyes and ears. Each of these individuals should be assigned to check on specific items and people. They must confirm that the items are in place and the people ready to proceed before you give permission for the curtain to go up. Here is a brief rundown of the types of assignments you might delegate to these different individuals.

Stage Manager

It is best to focus the stage manager's responsibilities on items that relate to the stage and backstage area. Here are some examples of what the stage manager should do:

- Check with the lighting crew to make sure that the stage lights have been tested and extra bulbs are available.
- Check with the tech crew to make sure the communications system has been tested and that replacement batteries are available for the lead actors' microphones.
- Check with the prop master to verify that all required props

are in place (all large scenery items should have been positioned and checked earlier that day).

- After making sure all these things are accounted for, the stage manager should then find you and personally report this to you.

Parents

Parent support is vital to the success of your show. See if you can recruit parent volunteers to be present and help out in the warm-up rooms one hour before curtain time. This additional adult supervision will make it possible for you and your colleagues to briefly leave your rooms if necessary to attend to any unexpected problems that may arise. Give each parent volunteer a specific room assignment at least a month in advance. If you can find two parents for each warm-up room, that is ideal. However, one parent to a room is also fine.

Teachers

Find one or two colleagues who are willing to visit the different warm-up rooms for you to verify that parent helpers you have assigned to those rooms and parents and other helpers scheduled to assist the lead actors with their makeup are actually present. If you have assigned two parents to each site and one of the two is not there, one parent in the room is enough. If both assigned parents are absent, the supervising teacher can go to a room where two parents are present and ask one to cover the problem room. The teacher should also make sure that the assigned VCR or DVD players make it to the warm-up rooms as scheduled. If the bathrooms near the rehearsal rooms are not open or have not been cleaned and equipped, the teacher should immediately report this to the custodian. Finally, if bottled water has been ordered for the rehearsal rooms, the teacher should make sure that the water has been delivered to all the rehearsal rooms. If the water has arrived at the school but has not been delivered to the appropriate rooms, the teacher should ask the custodian to take care of this as quickly as possible.

Administrators

Find out if there will be a school administrator present at every performance of the show. As soon as you know who will be assigned to each performance, ask those administrators to help you during the hour or so before the start of the show by making sure the ticket sellers, programs, and ushers are in place. Plan to have the administrator work together on this along with one of your most responsible parents. That way, if one of the two doesn't show up on time, you will still have someone there. If any of the ticket sellers, program distributors, or ushers does not arrive on time, the administrator and parent can use their judgment about how to keep things running smoothly. For example, in an emergency, they can ask students in the audience to serve as replacement ushers. If there is no one to distribute programs, they can put up a sign directing guests to take a printed program from a table in the lobby. If the ticket sellers do not materialize, either the parent or the administrator can take over that job until a replacement (teacher or parent) is found.

Ask the administrator well in advance if he or she would be willing to serve as the evening's MC. Most administrators will be pleased to do this. They will welcome the audience and introduce the show. At the conclusion, they will praise all the people involved in the show for their hard work and thank the audience for their support. By the way, it is politically savvy to have an administrator serve as your show's MC because it demonstrates to the students, teachers, parents, and audience members that your event enjoys the administration's support. In addition, it encourages the administrator to feel a greater connection to the show, which can be a good thing for you and your program.

LAST-MINUTE DETAILS

Have the individuals responsible for checking each of these items come back to see you prior to curtain time so you will know that each of these things has been completed. Keep a checklist for the night of the performance and make a mark next to each item once it has been reported to you. A sample checklist for the night of the performance is included in figure 6.1.

Name of Show: _____ Date of Show: _____

Time of show: _____ am/pm   Location: _____

Ticket Price: $ _____

Ticket sellers in place   _____

Programs placed near auditorium doors for distribution   _____

Ushers present   _____

MC ready   _____

Piano accompanist present   _____

Bathrooms open, cleaned, and well equipped   _____

Working water fountains/bottled water near warm-up rooms   _____

VCR or DVD players for warm-up rooms   _____

Parent helpers present at each warm-up room as assigned   _____

Parents and other helpers present to assist with makeup   _____

Stage lights tested   _____

Extra bulbs available   _____

Communication system tested   _____

Replacement batteries available for lead actors' microphones   _____

All required props are in place   _____

Figure 6.1.   Checklist for Performance

A SMOOTH EXIT

At the conclusion of each performance, directly after your MC's closing remarks, go to the microphone and direct all actors, chorus members, dancers, and band members to exit the stage and return to their assigned rooms. Remind parents that they can meet and retrieve their children in those rooms. This prevents unnecessary congestion in the auditorium after the performance.

CELEBRATION

Now that your students have savored the thrill of giving a success-ful performance, they are likely to remain in an excited state for a day or two. While high school students sometimes have cast parties following an evening performance, middle school students are a bit young to be staying out that late, especially if the next day is a school day. You may want to consider arranging a small celebration for everyone involved in the show on the next school day following the performance. Whether or not to do this is entirely up to you and not something you have to do.

If you decide to have the celebration, get parent volunteers to coordinate the purchase of party supplies well in advance and ar-range to have their expenses reimbursed through school funds. Don't forget to invite everyone involved in the show, including the principal and the custodians. If the students want to wear their costumes to the party, and you are agreeable, ask your principal for approval in advance.

Have the parents set up the food and drinks on long tables dur-ing the class period before the celebration is scheduled to begin. I used to invite everyone to the chorus room for these events. How-ever, you can hold the celebration anywhere in the school that is convenient and available.

Students and teachers retain many fond memories of a cast celebration. One year when I directed a middle school production of *South Pacific*, several parents approached me and asked if they could give the cast a party in the chorus room the day after the show. They took care of everything and, in addition, brought a big and delicious cake bearing the words, "Bravo, *South Pacific!*" That was a memorable celebration.

SUMMARY

Advance planning is a very important part of a successful middle school musical and its related unit of study. If you carefully plan and implement the logistical details for all the activities, you will avert potential conflicts among teachers, between teachers and the school administration, and between teachers and parents. Teachers and students will be better able to use their available rehearsal times to the best advantage. This will help to create a positive atmosphere and impart a feeling of confidence and comfort to everyone involved in the project.

Table 6.1. Timeline Countdown: Master Calendar

June	Week 2	Choral Director	Meet with colleagues to select the show for the following spring. Prepare all requests for performance rights/rentals.
September	Week 3	Choral Director, Dance, Theatre, Art, Band/Orch Teachers	Develop a plan addressing everyone's auditorium and scheduling needs.
		Choral Director	Send prepared requests.
	Week 4	Choral Director	Represent colleagues at a meeting with the principal to discuss scheduling and use of the auditorium during the spring semester.
October	Week 1	Choral Director	Select piano accompanists.
	Week 3	Choral Director	Contact area elementary schools and senior centers to arrange abbreviated performances for the month of May.
November	Week 2	Choral Director	Finalize all permissions. Give accompanists to the piano reduction to learn. Begin arranging solo and choral numbers for middle school voices.
		Band/Orchestra Director	Begin arranging the score to suit your available instrumentation and your students' abilities.
	Week 3	Choral Director	Work with colleagues to begin writing the unit of study.
		Theatre Teacher	Review script of show and make list of necessary props and costumes.
		Art Teacher	Measure auditorium and order basic supplies for scenery and stage set.

Table 6.1. (Continued)

November	Week 4	Dance Teacher and Choral Director	Begin to study the musical score and think about scenes that will require choreography.
		Choral Director	Get student newspaper to publicize dates and times of the show's spring performances.
December	Week 3	Choral Director	Finish arranging choral and solo numbers for middle school voices.
	Week 4	Band/Orchestra Director	Finish arranging instrumental numbers for available instruments.
		All Teachers	Complete writing the unit of study.
January	Week 1	All Teachers	Begin unit of study.
		Choral Director	Send a letter to parents re: audition details with tear-off for parents to sign and return giving their child permission to audition for a role.
	Week 2	Choral, Dance, and Theatre Teachers	Auditions.
		Choral Director and Office Staff	Send notes to selected students inviting them to callbacks.
		Volunteers (parents)	Begin to approach local businesses to solicit ads for the program.
	Week 3	Choral, Dance, and Theatre Teachers	Callbacks. Determine cast assignments.

Table 6.1. (Continued)

January	Week 4	Choral Director	Send letters to parents confirming final role assignments with tear-off for parents' approval and signature. Include information on rehearsal dates and times and solicit potential parent volunteers (see figure 4.1).
		Teachers in charge of crews	Identify members of each crew and meet with each crew to go over procedures and responsibilities.
		Choral, Dance, and Theatre Teachers	Begin working with the leading actors.
		Dance Teacher	Begin working with students on the choreography.
February	Week 1	Choral Director, Theatre Teacher	Review parent and colleague responses re: props, costumes, and volunteering.
	Week 2	Choral Director	Talk with parents who volunteered to determine what they might be best suited to help with. Make assignments.
	Weeks 3–4	Teachers in charge of crews	Each crew rehearses separately with the teacher in charge.
March	Week 1	Choral Director and Office Staff	Send letter to students, teachers, and parents announcing that it is time to purchase ads for the program (see figure 9.3).
	Week 3	Teachers	Formative assessment.
	Week 4	Choral Director, Office Staff, and Parent Volunteers	Enforce a deadline this week for the purchase of announcements in the program.
		Choral Director	Send information about show and complimentary tickets to local papers.

Table 6.1. (Continued)

April	Week 2	Office Staff	Print the program. If sending to an outside printer, allow additional time.
	Week 3	Choral Director	Send letter to parents re: dress rehearsal procedures and details for opening night.
May	Weeks 1–2	Choral Director and Teachers in charge of crews	Integrate each crew's activities into the combined rehearsals and then into the dress rehearsals.
	Week 2	Teachers in charge of crews, Theatre, Dance, and Choral Teachers	Separate rehearsal(s) for stage, tech, and lighting crews.
	Weeks 3–4	Everyone	Dress Rehearsal(s). Performance. Cast party. Abbreviated performances for elementary schools/senior centers.
		Teachers and Students	Summative assessment.
		Choral Director and Parents	Write thank-you notes and deliver copies of printed program to business sponsors.

7

ACTING, STAGE AND TECH CREW, AND CHOREOGRAPHY

How will you work with the student actors, supervise the stage and tech crews, and handle the choreography for your show simultaneously? I think it is best for the production and for the curricular unit of study if the music teacher can work in collaboration with a theatre educator and a dance educator. Some middle schools may have certified theatre arts and dance educators on staff with whom you can work. If your school does not have a theatre arts teacher you may be able to recruit an English teacher who has a background or interest in theatre. If you do not have a dance teacher in your school, try to find a dancer or dance teacher from the community to help out with the choreography.

But even if you are in a school or a location where there is simply no one else available to collaborate with, you can still work very effectively with your actors and dancers. This chapter will give you many ideas and suggestions and will also address issues related to supervising the stage and tech crews. Let's begin by talking about working with student actors.

WORKING WITH MIDDLE SCHOOL ACTORS

A good director thoroughly understands the musical's story, characters, and circumstances and effectively communicates that understanding to the students. Your actors need to become immersed in the story, learn how they fit into the story, and explore how their characters interact with one another. A skillful director helps students think about these things by posing questions such as, "What are the most important points in this scene?" or "What does your character want?"

The director needs to get students to feel comfortable on the stage. Theatre teachers have told me that while babies and young children are all natural actors, most people tend to become more inhibited and self-conscious as they grow older. One teacher even observed that her eighth graders always seem more inhibited than her seventh graders! Theatre teachers use a number of different strategies and techniques to get students comfortable onstage including theatre games, improvisation exercises, tableaux, and voice-projection games. The successful director helps student actors leave their natural feelings of awkwardness and self-consciousness behind so they can concentrate on becoming the characters they are portraying.

Theatre Games

Theatre games are relaxing, fun to play, and are usually very effective with middle school students. Once the students become absorbed in the games, they tend to forget about feeling self-conscious onstage. Tell them that these games aren't just for school and that they can play them any time they're together or teach them to their friends.

One popular theatre game involves an imaginary door. Tell the students that the door is about to open and that they're going to imagine what is behind that door and react to it. For example, if the students imagine that someone is threatening them, they'll need to back away. Or, if a good friend is behind the door, they can show pleasure and, maybe, hug the friend. This game sharpens students' reactions to surprises and helps student actors think about how their own moods and personalities change depending on the people they interact with. Each student actor gets a turn. The students watching the actors should try to guess what their reaction is. This feedback helps student actors determine how effective they are and introduces everyone to the emotional bond that forms between effective actors and an interested audience.

The mirror game, another type of theatre game, requires students to physically reflect the motions of a partner. Organize your students in pairs. One student in each pair, the leader, looks at the partner as if looking into a mirror. The second student is the leader's reflection in the mirror and must reflect exactly every motion the leader makes. After a while, have the students reverse roles. The goal of this game is for the students to focus so intently and communicate so closely that there is no time lag between the leader's motions and the follower's reflection. The two students should be so connected that an observer would have difficulty distinguishing between the leader and the follower. This game prepares students to focus on other characters during a performance.

Improvisation Exercises

Middle school students have great imaginations and enjoy improvisation exercises. Play an improvisation game with your students by giving the group a situation, an opening line, and a closing line. For example, tell the students to imagine they are standing on top of the Empire State Building. Let's say you give them an opening line, "Don't jump!" and a closing line, "Oh! You look great!" Then, ask the students to improvise a scene based on those suggestions. Once the students learn the game, you can ask them to come up with their own situations, opening lines, and closing lines.

Another effective improvisation exercise requires students to tell a story as a group. The story can be one that they create on the spot or it can be a story they already know. The teacher selects one student to begin the story. At some point the teacher points to another student who must now take over with no gap and continue to tell the story. This exercise continues until everyone has had an opportunity to relate part of the story. In order to successfully play this game, the students need to focus intently on listening to the story as it develops. They have to be able to jump in at any time without a pause and continue the tale from the last word spoken by the previous student.

Theater Games for the Classroom: A Teacher's Handbook, and *Improvisation for the Theater: A Handbook of Teaching and Directing Techniques,* both by Viola Spolin, are excellent sources of additional theatre games and improvisation exercises.

Create Tableaux Onstage

One theatre teacher feels that, since middle school students can be quite excitable and energetic, it is important to give them a specific structure for developing a sense of where they are onstage in relation to each other during a scene. He uses an exercise where a group of four or five students creates a story and physically tells the story by creating eight frozen pictures onstage. These frozen pictures, also called tableaux, give the students a good idea of where they physically need to be on the stage at those different points in the scene. Once the students begin to act out the scene, the tableaux they created earlier will serve as helpful reference points for the students' physical location onstage.

The same teacher explained to me how he and his students created tableaux for a scene taken from an adaptation of *Gulliver's Travels.* The scene portrayed goofy scholars in a nonsense academy displaying their inventions. The students and teacher identified several group movements, along with some transitions and individual movements that would constitute the tableaux. The tableaux portrayed all the scholars raising their arms in a "ta-dah" gesture, walking five paces, bowing, spinning in a circle, clustering in a group, breaking apart, and, finally, each student performing an original "strut."

The concept of creating tableaux can also be useful when working with musical numbers in the show. Let's say you are directing *Little Shop of Horrors* and want your students to devise tableaux for the song "Downtown," which takes place in Act One, Scene One. The script calls for "Downtown" to be sung by three girl urchins along with three of the lead actors (Audrey, Seymour, and Mr. Mushnik). The three urchins function as a sort of Greek chorus with attitude. Their singing style mirrors that of 1960s girl groups. I arranged the song to include vocal parts for students in my larger chorus so that they could sing along with the urchins. Here's how to do it: Place the larger chorus in various positions around the stage, with the three urchins mobile and the large chorus relatively stationary. Ask the three girls to work independently to come up with five pictures. Then, incorporate those pictures into the movements they'll make during the song.

For example, the lyrics to "Downtown" mention traveling uptown to clean rich people's homes. Perhaps the girls could begin the number in a horizontal formation. That could be the first picture. For the second picture, Mr. Mushnik could join the girls as they fan out across the stage in a vain attempt to hail cabs to get uptown. For the third picture, each girl might move to a different location onstage, pantomiming cleaning someone's home, while Audrey comes out of the flower shop and sits on top of a garbage can. In the fourth picture, the girls might suddenly kneel and face the flower shop where Seymour sings, "Someone, show me a way to get outa here!" For the final picture, the three girls could resume the girl group lineup they began with.

These examples represent only one possible series of tableaux for "Downtown." Empower your students to devise their own tableaux, which will tap their creative energy and will keep them constructively occupied while you work with other cast members.

Your students will come up with some great ideas you might never have thought of!

Voice Projection

Most middle school students need to work on projecting their voices so that they can be heard in a large space. Try placing one student onstage and another in the back row of the house. Have them carry on a conversation with each other using normal, shouting, and stage voices. This teaches them to throw their voices. Before each rehearsal, ask the group to imagine opening night, when the auditorium will be full of people. Tell them they have to be heard by the people in the back row. Ask your students to pretend that their grandmother or grandfather is hard-of-hearing and sitting in the back row. The students will have to project their voices and enunciate clearly so they can be heard by their grandparents.

Teach your students to think of sound as something that occupies space. This image helps students to focus more on the sound they make. Viola Spolin suggests that you have your actors practice "sending" their sound back and forth to each other across the stage. Play a game by having two or more students sit on the stage at a distance from one another. Each player should send a sound to his/her partner. Then, have each student onstage send a sound to each of the other players. Finally, let all the students send sounds to each other in a give-and-take style.

Working with Students Who Overact or Play Their Part for Laughs

Some students just seem to overact all the time. Their delivery of lines and their body language often appear exaggerated. Try to determine why they are overcompensating. Some students may be genuinely concerned that they are not being heard or understood. You can say to those students, "You don't need to try so hard" or,

"Relax! Your character is coming across very well." These positive and reassuring comments are more constructive and will be more effective than saying something like, "Don't overact!"

Other students may simply be natural "hams" who play every line for laughs and love to "mug" for the audience. Often they will face the audience directly, ignoring the other actors onstage. Many of these students would probably do well as stand-up comics. But as one middle school theatre teacher observed, "When you are working for an ensemble approach, these antics stand out like a sore thumb." What can you do to make this a less likely occurrence in your productions? What do you do when it happens anyway?

Before rehearsing for a show, emphasize the importance of working as an ensemble. One teacher tells his students, "We are all here together with a single focus. Every piece of acting you do should fit into a greater whole." Help your students to understand that actions that don't support the team effort take away from the larger picture. Remind them that they need to relate to the other actors onstage, not to the audience.

When you first notice an actor playing for laughs, try to tone the student down diplomatically. You might say something like, "Pretend your character is not feeling well today." If the student persists, explain that a *real* actor plays the character and that *real* comedy comes from the character, not from the person who's playing the character. Ask questions such as "Who is this person you are playing?" and ask the actors to describe how their characters might react to certain situations. Once the actors focus on playing their characters, they will usually stop playing for laughs. You can also let these students view their performances on videotape. This may help them to see that they are overplaying a role.

However, there will always be some tough cases. I had a student in a production of *South Pacific* whom we cast as Luther Billis, the entrepreneurial sailor with a big heart who always manages to get himself in trouble. It seemed a perfect fit, since our student's exuberance, slyness, and bravado was vintage Luther Billis. Also, like Billis, our student was no stranger to trouble.

Even after we worked with him to try to get him to play the character, he still often went over the top and resorted to mugging. So we decided to set very strict parameters for him. We complimented him immediately when he played the character correctly or did something great (which he often did). We also made it clear when he did something inappropriate and forced him to fix the problem right then. Naturally, it might have saved us time and aggravation to simply remove this student from the cast. However, he did have talent, and we felt that a middle school musical should be a growth experience for everyone involved. So we continued to work with him. In the end, our Luther Billis gave a marvelous performance. We even let him loose a bit in the "Honey Bun" number, where some mugging and exaggeration can actually be helpful.

Nurture the Shy Students

When you are seriously considering a student for a role, you've probably already noticed something about the student that makes him or her a good fit for the part. But what if the student is shy? Can you risk giving the role to a shy student?

It is often harder to draw out the acting abilities of a shy student than to tone down a ham. Initially, shy students can appear inhibited, fearful of trying new things, and often soft spoken.

Unfortunately these students are sometimes passed over at auditions and are often not given acting roles.

Don't be afraid of casting a shy student if that student seems right for a particular role. You can find creative ways to bring out the student's acting abilities. In fact, some theatre teachers believe that the shy students often have the most active and lively imaginations. Remember that imagination is a big part of acting. Help these students use their imaginations to take the focus off themselves and transfer it to building their character. For example, suggest an image for students to focus on that will cause them to react physically and emotionally as the character would, or give them a small prop they can keep on their person that they can use to help define their character.

One teacher was working with a shy girl who had a role in a production adapted from *Tales of the Arabian Nights*. The teacher embellished the part, giving the character an "in-your-face" personality and a strong Brooklyn accent. The student became so absorbed in creating this unusual character that she had no time to be shy. The Brooklyn accent became an imaginative mental prop for her to work with and helped her overcome her shyness onstage.

To help a shy boy cast as a prisoner in the Bastille during a production of *Tale of Two Cities*, the same teacher gave the boy a cane to use. This physical prop stimulated the actor's imagination and helped him build his character, drawing him out of his shyness. Another teacher told me about a situation where a female character needed to react strongly to another actor who was saying things that were extremely painful for the first one to hear. However, the student wasn't reacting as if the words were hurting her. According to the teacher, "The director told her to imagine that every time the (other) actor opened her mouth, fire or flames would come out and nearly burn her. That simple image gave the actress the motivation to cover her face, and to turn her face away. It worked, and yet the audience was not aware that she was using this technique."

A middle school theatre teacher I have worked with sums it up this way: "The actor who is shy can often give a truly realistic performance, heartfelt, and moving. The shy actor can find a voice and very often move an audience to tears because of the simple, bare-bones approach to a role."

Blocking

In her book, *Way Off Broadway*, Lynne M. Soeby explains that, "In a musical, blocking includes all un-choreographed movement of actors" (Soeby, 1991, p. 80). After reviewing the script, you will want to think about how your actors will move about onstage as they interact with each other. The principles of blocking presented here are essentially the same as those you'd use with any theatre group, professional or amateur.

Three-Quarter Stance Some students will naturally want to face the audience in full frontal position. With some exceptions, this is not appropriate in theatre. Have them learn to adopt what is called a three-quarter stance: the downstage foot set back about a foot and the upstage foot about a foot ahead. This way, the students onstage appear as if they are talking to the actors they are facing, but are also lending their body to the audience. The three-quarter stance is a standard practice that directors and actors use all the time.

Movement As one actor speaks to another, the speaking actor crosses so that the action onstage does not appear to be static. When the actor turns back, he or she moves downstage so that the actor's back is not turned toward the audience. Actors who are not speaking shouldn't move while another actor is speaking. If they move, it will take the focus off the speaker. Never have another actor move past or otherwise block the speaker.

Sightlines Always be aware of sightlines when planning your blocking. Every member of the audience must be able to see the action onstage. For example, think about the audience member who is sitting very far stage left, almost next to the wall. If all your actors are center stage, this person will not be able to see the center speaker because the actor to the left will block the view. One way to solve this problem is to place the actors in a triangle so that one character is left, one is right, and the speaker is center. The sightlines are no longer blocked, and that audience member can now see everyone onstage.

As you run your rehearsals, make a point of sitting in different sections of the auditorium in order to spot other potential sightline problems. Perhaps there are large props or parts of the scenery that could restrict certain audience members' views of the action onstage. If so, adjust the placement of these materials.

Finally, make sure that backstage goings-on are not visible to your audience. Remember to use as much of the stage as possible so the action doesn't appear static or confined to one area. Always think of the full picture.

Flexibility Come to rehearsal prepared with your ideas for each scene. However, this doesn't mean that you can't be flexible as the rehearsal progresses. For example, if a student improvises a movement you think is good, you can certainly include it in your plan for the scene. Also, if you have previously asked your students to create tableaux for a particular scene and it seems to work, go ahead and build the scene around these. This is an excellent way of involving your students in the blocking process.

Working with Large Groups

If one of the actors is speaking to a large crowd onstage, put the members of the crowd on different levels. The speaker can be placed on a platform looking down at the crowd and facing full front (this is one of the few exceptions to the rule that prohibits an actor from facing full front). This configuration is used in the play *Our Town*, during the wedding and funeral scenes where the stage manager, placed front center stage, speaks to a large crowd positioned to the side facing him.

When you have a crowd scene, tell the members of the crowd that even though their faces may not always be visible to the audience, they can still act with their arms, backs, and shoulders. Encourage each student in the crowd to develop an individual identity and to express that identity through physical actions and body language. Crowd members should keep their roles in perspective so that they don't "steal the show." Also, unless indicated in the script, crowd members should never take the focus away from the speakers by talking to each other.

STAGE AND TECH CREWS

Students who want to be involved in the musical but who are not comfortable performing onstage can work on the stage crew, tech crew, or lighting crew. (We'll talk about the stage and tech crews in this chapter and the lighting crew in chapter 8.) Schedule a time to meet with students who may be interested in joining a crew. Get a sense of their background and experience and try to determine the best assignment for each child. To ensure that there will be a balance of veterans and newcomers on crews every year, make sure that your crews contain students representing every grade level.

Recruit interested teachers or exceptionally talented and responsible students to supervise the stage and tech crews. Many middle schools already have a teacher who runs the audio/visual squad. That person might be a good choice to train the tech crew and supervise the communications system.

Stage Crew

No prior experience is necessary to become a member of the stage crew. Students in the stage crew usually develop a close rapport and team spirit. Stage crew members traditionally wear black, which makes them easy to identify and ensures that they remain inconspicuous when changing scenery. One middle school theatre arts teacher always gives his stage crew the following pep talk: "You're a very important part of this show. One of the things we're going to do is dress in black, black tights, black shirts, nothing bright because we're going to go in during the blackouts and change the scenery. You're going to move the scenery and props; we're going to rehearse this."

Rehearse the stage crew separately until these students can do scene changes quickly and quietly so as not to disrupt the mood of the show. Then, combine the stage crew with the tech and lighting crews for several technical rehearsals, without any actors. During the second to last week of general rehearsals, combine the crews with the entire cast for technical rehearsals so the crew members can practice integrating their work with the rhythm of the show. For the final week, everyone should be involved in every general rehearsal.

It is important to tape down any loose wires onstage with fluorescent tape so the stage crew and actors can see them in the dark. That way, no one will trip over those wires during scene changes. In addition, put the same fluorescent tape on the edge of any steps that the stage crew or actors may have to climb (either as part of the stage set or the actual steps leading up to the stage), so that these will also be illuminated when the lights go out.

If a standing prop such as a sofa or lamp will have to be moved during a scene change when the lights are down, put fluorescent tape on the floor to mark the location of these props. For example, mark the spots where each of the four sofa legs should go. If the prop will remain onstage for the entire show, you do not need to mark it with fluorescent tape. Use regular tape instead so the stage crew knows where to place the prop prior to the start of the show.

During scene changes when the stage is dark, actors can signal the stage manager or members of the stage crew by snapping their fingers or by making a clicking sound with their tongues. For example, once the stage crew completes a scene change and the actors are in place, these sounds can be used to let the stage manager know to bring up the lights for the new scene.

Many teachers group students in pairs and assign each pair to perform specific tasks. For example, one pair may be assigned to open and close the curtains while another pair will be in charge of sweeping the floor. Another middle school teacher remarked, "Being on the stage crew seems like so much fun that the actors sometimes try to help move the flats. I have to remind the actors that is not their job."

Middle school teachers hold differing opinions about the value of choosing one student to be stage manager. Some teachers are comfortable with this practice and say that the stage manager's assistance is invaluable. Other teachers would rather not create a situation that might encourage overly aggressive or bossy behavior. In any case, there will always be mature, responsible students whom you can depend on to help you on either a formal or informal basis.

Find a Reliable Prop Master   You will definitely need a prop master for each performance. If you are double casting, use one prop master for each cast. Select your most reliable students for the job of prop master. Explain to them that they must make sure that the correct props are placed onstage on time for each scene.

Prop masters are responsible for all light, portable materials called for in the show that do not need to be transported by the stage crew. Examples of props might be a piece of jewelry, a letterhead, or a book. The prop master makes a checklist of all props needed for the show in order of appearance. He or she goes over the list directly before the show and again during the show, crossing off each item on the list once it has been placed onstage.

One middle school theatre teacher illustrated the importance of the prop master by telling students what happened to him during a community theatre production of John Patrick's *The Curious Savage*, where a teddy bear prop was needed in the second act. Someone forgot to put the teddy bear onstage and the bear's presence was critical to the dialogue. One actor, improvising in exasperation, said, "I thought the teddy bear was here!" Another said, "Yes! Has anybody seen the teddy bear?" All of a sudden, someone threw the teddy bear onto the stage from the wings. The teacher then explained to the students that this is the sort of experience they wanted to avoid.

Recruit an Effective Stage Manager A good stage manager can help ensure that your show runs smoothly. Stage managers help the director coordinate the many details involved in a production by communicating with the actors and the stage, tech, and lighting crew. The student you select as stage manager does not have to come from the theatre or choral program. One teacher I know found someone in her general music class who became an outstanding stage manager. See if you can recruit someone responsible, respected by his or her peers, and a natural leader.

You may want to meet with your stage manager for a few minutes every day, perhaps around lunchtime, to go over what is needed for afternoon, evening, or the next morning's rehearsals. During these daily meetings, remind the stage manager of the scenes you plan to rehearse, the kind of lighting you'll need, what props to put in place or have ready, and which microphones will need to be set up and where. Make sure your stage manager carries a clipboard, pencil, and paper to these meetings, so he or she can take good notes. The stage manager should then relay this information to the relevant crews and to the prop master.

The position of stage manager is a critical one. If your stage manager is proving to be ineffective or unreliable, do not hesitate to replace that student with someone else.

Tech Crew

The tech crew is in charge of the sound system. As in the stage crew, membership in the tech crew can be open to anyone. Because of the very precise nature of this job, some middle school directors require that tech crew members maintain a record of 100 percent attendance at rehearsals.

The tech crew usually joins the regular rehearsals about two weeks before opening night. In general, try to limit membership in the tech crew to no more than fifteen students. As with the stage crew, middle school teachers often assign two students to each task so that if one student forgets something, the other may remember. For example, pairs of students can be assigned backstage to follow specific singers and actors. When these individuals go onstage, the crew members hand them the correct microphones, and when they go backstage, the crew members turn off the microphones. These pairs of students could also be responsible for minor emergencies involving their actors' microphones such as adjusting the placement or replacing the batteries if they fell out while the actors were onstage.

If your school has a computerized soundboard, other crew members might be assigned to set up computer-generated cues for some of the different sound effects needed during the course of the musical. For example, two of the required sound effects in *West Side Story* are church bells and gunshots. If you have a computerized system, your students can take the specific sounds they need from sound effect CDs, which can be purchased at a store like Target or online. You can buy sound effect CDs containing many random sounds or CDs specializing in specific sounds such as musical instruments or animals. Tech crew members can then edit the desired sound on their sound system's computer to the specifications needed.

Of course, many schools do not have computerized sound systems, and you may need to work with a system that is older and less sophisticated. Often an older sound system contains an amplifier, CD, or tape player; speakers; and a combination of standing and portable microphones. You can still play sound effects on a CD player, assuming you either custom edit the sound effects elsewhere or find a sound effects CD that gives you what you need without editing. However, you and your students can also find other creative ways to produce sound effects. For example, to get the sound effect of gunshots for *West Side Story* one of your students could fire a toy gun near an offstage microphone. Another student could strike a large bell backstage near another offstage microphone to simulate the sound of a church bell.

Communication Systems   It is vital to have some kind of communication system in place so that directors can talk to members of their crews during rehearsals and performances. Some schools may have a "Clear-Com" system; others use walkie-talkies. A Clear-Com system is basically a telephone in a box (newer versions come with a headset or earpiece). If the light on the phone blinks, it means someone is calling you and you need to pick up the phone. These are stationary phones; they are not portable.

Many directors at the middle school level communicate with the members of the tech crew via a walkie-talkie system. If using walkie-talkies, buy the same model for everyone on the crew. Walkie-talkies can be purchased as headsets with an earpiece and a built in microphone for speaking so that your hands can be free at all times. This works well for all crew members. In addition, performers and audience members will never be distracted by your incoming messages since only you will be able to hear them.

Whether you use Clear-Com or walkie-talkie systems, you should have a station in the light booth, at the soundboard, backstage, and one for the advisor. Crew members may be tempted to chat with other crew members using the system. Emphasize to the students that they are not to talk on this system unless there is an emergency. If you have a student who is familiar with the sound system and is a natural leader, consider making this student the head of the tech crew.

DELEGATE RESPONSIBILITY

A good director knows how to delegate responsibility. Remember that you are working with students who want to demonstrate how mature and grown-up they can be. Take advantage of this trait and give promising students positions of responsibility. Jobs as prop master, stage manager, and leadership positions on the various crews can all be offered to the appropriate individuals. As your students assume greater responsibility for various aspects of the production, they will increasingly feel that the show is theirs. You will be surprised at how seriously they take the jobs you have given them. In the end, they will learn not just how to perform a musical, but also how to take responsibility and achieve success as important members of a team.

CHOREOGRAPHY

We all know from personal experience that middle school students can be physically awkward and extremely self-conscious about their appearance. The idea of dancing may turn off many of the boys. Girls may be embarrassed by the appearance of their toes when dancing barefoot. Girls may also resist suggestions to pull back their hair for dancing, believing that this will make their faces look less attractive. How can you motivate these students to get excited and confident about dancing? What kinds of choreography can you devise for them?

First, think of choreography as the motion of bodies in space, not as "dance steps." This will help you and the students move beyond any fears of inadequacy you may have about "dancing." When your audience looks at choreography onstage, they see formations of bodies and patterns of movement. Your primary purpose should be to create movement patterns that help the students look good onstage. Determine what your students are capable of doing and what they feel comfortable doing. For example, can they walk and move their arms at the same time? If not, the movements you devise should include one or the other, not both. Even just walking can be very effective for large groups onstage. When the students realize that your goal is to make them look great onstage, you will have taken the first step toward building their confidence and trust.

Involve the Students in Creating the Choreography

You can continue to build trust by letting the students help you create the choreography. When you show the students that you value their ideas, they will feel that the resulting choreography is "theirs." For example, one middle school dance teacher explained how she worked with her students to devise choreography based on the theme of snow. First, she had the students brainstorm words related to snow. Then, asking the students to act out those words, she selected some of their movements and helped the students to physically expand these ideas. For example, some students demonstrated shoveling. The teacher encouraged the students to expand their portrayal of *shoveling* to include the motions of both digging and reaching. She then worked with another motion the students had created to the word *shivering* and helped them connect the two ideas. In other words, the teacher helped the students build a sequence of movements. Building a sequence of movements is the basis of choreography. Her students felt that they "owned" this choreography because they helped create it.

Another dance teacher described how she elicited ideas from her students when choreographing a scene from *Guys and Dolls*. In this scene, Sky Masterson takes Sarah Brown to Havana in order to win a bet he made with his friends that he could get her to fall in love with him. Sarah drinks too much and gets into a fight with other patrons at a nightclub. The teacher got her students involved in exploring possible ideas for movement by asking questions. For example, she asked whether the bar patrons should be sitting or standing at the bar and how the fight should begin. She also listened to her students' ideas about how to represent fighting in the dance, how the other characters should react to the fight, and who should get into the fight and how. This is another example of how a teacher was able to build student trust and confidence by involving them in creating and structuring the resulting dance.

Get the Boys to Dance

What are some strategies you can use to get the boys to dance? Dance teachers who have worked with middle school students suggest making it clear from the beginning that "We are not calling this 'dance.'" Next, make choreography that features the boys as athletic as possible. Involve the boys in creating the movements they will be performing.

One dance teacher talked about the difficulty she encountered with her boys when choreographing a particular scene from *Once upon a Mattress*. The script called for several of the male characters to line up and, one at a time, present themselves to the princess. The boys were awkward and self-conscious, and the scene wasn't working well. The teacher decided to try a different approach. She asked each boy to show her one thing he could do that was "spectacular." One boy slid into first base. Another did a double split. A third boy jumped as if reaching for a basketball shot. The teacher incorporated these things into the choreography so that each boy would have his own starring moment. The boys' motivation increased dramatically and the routine turned out to be very successful.

The dance teacher working on *Guys and Dolls* shared an anecdote about her experience working with the boys when choreographing the crapshoot scene. In order to get the boys to shed their inhibitions, she told them that they would be creating a "boy dance." She took care to make sure that the movements appeared as masculine as possible, incorporating jumps, runs, and walking steps. For example, when rolling the dice, the boys knelt down on one knee. If the dice produced a winning number, the boy rolling the dice would slap his knee in joy. If the result was bad, the boy might hop up, spin, or jump back, indicating disappointment. The teacher explained that the resulting choreography incorporated a lot of acting, not just dancing. The success of the routine relied a lot on the characters' reactions to the rolling of the dice. The teacher also mentioned that she always made a habit of cultivating good relationships with the popular boys in the school, especially the respected athletes. Once those boys became involved in the choreography, others followed.

Which Students Should Dance?

Avoid having your dancers sing and dance at the same time. It is enough for them to focus on the movement alone.

Many teachers at the middle school level believe that it is appropriate to work with any student who is interested in being involved in the dancing. This is consistent with the middle school philosophy of emphasizing exploration as opposed to specialization. Even if you have some students who are less than graceful, you can always find ways to incorporate them into the dance routines. Being onstage is important to them, and they will remember this experience for many years to come.

Other middle school teachers hold auditions in order to select a core group of dancers for the show. If you are auditioning potential dancers, it is a good idea to go through some warm-up exercises first and then teach everyone part of a simple to moderately difficult routine from one of the show's numbers. Once the students have learned the movements, have them perform the routine in groups of five or six and rate them on their performance. Even teachers who hold auditions will usually accept a really motivated student, even if he or she is not as adept as the others.

Rehearsing with Dancers

The dancers need plenty of time to rehearse their routines separately, apart from general cast rehearsals. The right time to bring the dancers into the general rehearsals is usually a few weeks prior to the performance. At that time, you'll want to emphasize transitions. For example, make sure your dancers know where they should be before the scene where they dance and where they go after the scene ends.

Safety Issues

Before beginning separate rehearsals for the dancers, you should already know where the set and props will eventually be located on the stage. Mark these locations and remind your dancers repeatedly. For example, if there will be a couch onstage, you should create a footprint of a couch from a roll of paper and write "couch" on it with a large black marker. If the dancers are not made aware of these things from the beginning, they may end up bumping into scenery and props when they perform later.

Know the size of your stage's wing space. If the wings are shallow, avoid having dancers exit the stage running full speed into the wings. They may be unable to stop in time and could injure themselves by running into a wall. Even if you have more wing space, you should still station people in the wings to gently stop the dancers' momentum with outstretched hands. This could be done by members of a student stage crew, or better yet, by adults assigned to the wings. These and other safety issues to consider when producing a musical are listed in figure 7.1, which you can use as a checklist.

Costumes and Footwear for Dancing

In general, it is a good idea to keep dancers' costumes as simple and comfortable as possible. It is essential for the students to become comfortable moving in their costumes; your dancers should always rehearse wearing the same type of outfits they will eventually perform in. For example, if the girls will wear dresses or skirts

Things to Do

Know and observe your school's fire regulations. _____

Make sure every flat item used as scenery has a jack or similar support behind it. _____

Place a stage weight, such as a sandbag, on top of the jack for extra support. _____

Tape down any loose wires onstage with fluorescent tape. _____

Mark edges of steps leading to stage (or part of stage set) with fluorescent tape. _____

Mark and label areas onstage that will contain props and elements of stage set. _____

Inspect auditorium floor before every rehearsal/performance. _____

Remove any nails sticking out of auditorium floor. _____

Request that the custodians ensure there is no water on auditorium floor and that the floor is swept clean before every rehearsal and performance. _____

Have dancers rub soles of new dance shoes with sandpaper to prevent slipping. _____

Assign adults to the stage wings to stop momentum of exiting dancers. _____

Make sure there is adequate ventilation in auditorium and warm-up rooms. _____

Arrange for nurse's office to be open and staffed on the nights of performance. _____

Arrange for security guard to be present on nights of performance. _____

Things to Avoid

Waxing auditorium floor. _____

Using glossy or spray paint when students are present. _____

Placing plastic or other flammable materials near theatre lights. _____

Allowing students to climb ladders or work with electrical wires. _____

Allowing students to do any carpentry work (unless as part of an industrial arts class supervised by a certified industrial arts teacher). _____

Figure 7.1. Safety Guidelines

for the performance, they need to rehearse in those same dresses or skirts from the beginning. If the actual dresses or skirts are not ready during rehearsal times, the girls need to wear substitute dresses or skirts of similar length and style for rehearsal.

The best shoes to wear for dancing are those that have traction. If the choreography mostly involves walking and/or running, sneakers are acceptable. Jazz or character shoes, which generally cost between thirty and sixty dollars a pair, are also good. When the shoes are new, rub the soles with sandpaper to make them less slippery. Avoid shoes that may be too slippery, such as ballet slippers. If your students are economically disadvantaged, it is good to know that many discount stores sell slippers with a harder sole that conforms to the shape of the feet. Some teachers have their dancers all wear either black socks or socks peds. Socks peds are little, soft socks with a very low ankle and rubber on the bottom. They look like the feet of children's pajamas, only more rubberized. Whatever the case, students' footwear should be uniform.

Flooring

If your school already has an established dance program, chances are that the students are rehearsing and performing on what is called a "sprung" floor. This is a wood floor specifically built to give a little when you jump on it. A sprung floor is essential for a dance program, since repetitive jumping on a nonsprung floor can result in students getting shin splints. If your school has no dance program, your auditorium does not have a sprung floor, and your choreography involves relatively simple, everyday movements, you should not have any problem using the facilities that exist. Some teachers like to put down mats with foam underneath, generically known as marleys, to cushion a hard floor. You can get more information about sprung floors and marley floors from dance flooring companies such as Harlequin Floors (www.harlequinfloors.com) or Stage Step (www.stagestep.com).

Regardless of where they dance, dancers must have a smooth surface to work on. Always inspect the floor before rehearsing or performing to make sure that there are no nails sticking out of the floor. Any exposed nails should be hammered down or covered prior to using the stage. Make sure the floor is swept clean before every rehearsal. Avoid waxing the floor. A waxed floor is too slippery for dancing and is considered a safety hazard.

How Can Music Teachers Learn to Work with Dancers?

First, don't be intimidated by the idea of choreography. Think of choreography for middle school musicals as motion in space instead of "dance steps." Consider taking a Dalcroze class. The Dalcroze approach emphasizes learning music through movement and will develop your skills and confidence. Many community music schools as well as area college and university music departments offer Dalcroze classes. You can also apply the skills you learn in this class to your methods of teaching classroom music. In addition, you may want to take a class in movement for the theatre, beginning jazz dance, or beginning modern dance. Any of these classes will give you a basic understanding of how to express yourself through movement.

Find a videotape of the musical theatre or movie version of the show you are thinking of presenting and watch it several times. Observe the patterns of how people are moving onstage. Don't copy the exact patterns you see on the tape; remember that this is someone else's choreography and that it was designed for professional/adult dancers.

It is better to create your own movement patterns. You may find instances where ballroom dancing is required for specific musical numbers. For example, in "Shall We Dance," from *The King and I*, the two lead characters perform a polka. In "Hernando's Hideaway," from *The Pajama Game*, the ensemble performs a tango. If

you choose to produce a musical that incorporates ballroom dancing, it is important not to substitute different dance styles for the
original numbers but to use the exact dance that is called for. As
an example, it would not be authentic to choreograph scenes from
Grease to hip-hop music because hip-hop music was not around in
the 1950s.

There are numerous resources you can use to learn and then
teach specific dances and dance styles. One such resource is
Dancetime Publications (dancetimepublications.com), which offers a series of instructional DVDs spanning five hundred years of
dance history. Each DVD covers a particular era and style (e.g.,
ragtime, Victorian Era, Renaissance). The DVDs provide step-by-
step instruction in several dance forms of the particular era and
offer accompanying information about the history of those dances.

SUMMARY

This chapter was designed to give you some basic information
about working with student actors, dancers, and members of stage
and tech crews. The ideas and strategies we discussed will help you
whether you are working directly with these aspects of the show or
just supervising these areas. In the next chapter, we will look at
other aspects of the musical that are not always familiar to musicians: scenery, stage sets, costumes, makeup, and lighting.

8

SCENERY, SET DESIGN AND CONSTRUCTION, COSTUMES, MAKEUP, AND LIGHTING

The first step in creating your show's stage set and scenery is to give teachers and students the opportunity to talk about and develop a shared vision of how the stage should look. In order to get some ideas, everyone should read and discuss the script as well as any work of literature that may have influenced the script. For example, if you are presenting *The King and I*, read and discuss both the libretto and the book *Anna and the King of Siam*, by Anna Leonowens, which inspired the libretto. Leonowens's book contains many vivid and colorful descriptions of the palace, the native trees and plants, the temples, and the room where she taught her classes. These descriptions can inspire everyone's imaginations and motivate students and teachers to create beautiful and expressive scenery and stage sets.

The art teacher can share examples of pictures, paintings, or photographs that can help students and teachers get a clearer sense of the world the show takes place in. Is that world cold or warm, sunny or gloomy? What colors are prominent? What do the houses look like and what materials are they made of? What do the trees and plants look like?

It is also very important to develop a sense of what the play will look like onstage. One way of doing this is to create a storyboard.

Students imagine a visual setting for each scene of the musical, and a designated student translates the ideas into a sketch on the board. These sketches can suggest what the eventual stage sets might look like. If you try this approach, don't limit your ideas to images from prior productions or movies. There is never only one correct image of a set for a particular show. In fact, you can produce the same show many times over the years using a different set design concept each time.

From a curricular standpoint, and also to establish a fair division of labor, it is best for the school's art teacher and art students to handle the scenery and set design. However, if your school does not have an art teacher or program, try to get an artist from the community, an interested colleague, or a college student majoring in art and design to supervise the hands-on art activities, following the suggestions in this chapter. Identify the students in your school who have an interest in art and recruit them. Middle school students, when motivated, are capable of working hard. They will get the job done.

COORDINATING STUDENT ASSIGNMENTS

An effective way of determining student roles and assignments for working on backdrop and scenery is to ask for their preferences. Some students will want to be actively involved in painting the backdrop or designing the scenery. Others may prefer a helping role such as being in charge of giving out water and brushes. Still others may want to be involved in documenting the entire work in progress or overseeing one of the aspects of the work. The more you honor the students' preferences, the more motivated the students will be. It is a good practice to have students work in small groups. Each group should be self-sufficient. Try to include one or two strong leaders in each group.

SCENERY

Effective scenery visually transports the audience to the place and time of the story by suggesting specific characteristics of the world the characters inhabit. The scenery you create should take the ideas and suggestions that came out of the initial discussions and incorporate these into a large picture onstage. This can be a challenging task in a large school auditorium, since what happens onstage can sometimes appear very small. Start by filling the height and width of your auditorium's rear wall with a large and colorful backdrop. Then, try to arrange the scenery to suggest different levels of height. These two strategies will help you create that large picture.

Design the Backdrop

Middle school art teachers generally paint the backdrop on either a piece of heavyweight muslin, rolled-out canvas paper, or even on bed sheets if no other material is available. Muslin is a flame-resistant material that is available at many fabric stores. Because muslin is thin and susceptible to cracking and curling, teachers recommend using heavyweight muslin. See if you can find a piece on sale or find a discontinued piece at a fabric store. Muslin is sold in many different sizes, so be sure to measure the height and length of your backstage wall before you go shopping. Some art stores may be willing to create the size you need. To prevent the muslin from curling, run a metal wire or sew a chain through the bottom.

You and your students will need uninterrupted time in the auditorium to paint the backdrop. First, protect the floor by covering it with heavyweight plastic. Secure the plastic to the floor with tape so that the plastic surface is completely flat and smooth. Then, lay the muslin over the plastic and tape it to the plastic. The muslin should now lie flat and smooth over the plastic.

The next step in the process is to use a primer, just as if you were painting a wall in your house. Many art teachers recommend using latex flat paint, such as house paint, for the primer. Avoid using gesso because it can cause the muslin to crack. Generally it is best to use white as a primer. However, if your scenery will be mostly sky (not white), you can save time by using your sky color as the primer. You'll need several coats of primer; each coat will need several hours to dry. Dilute the first two coats with one-half to one-third water. The paint should now be the consistency of milk. Apply the primer to the muslin with black foam disposable brushes or rollers. Most of the first coat of primer is absorbed directly into the muslin and is hardly visible. Continue the process. The third layer should not be diluted.

After the third layer of primer dries, you can start painting the actual colors. Many middle school teachers like to work with their students to apply the primer. The teachers then lay out the design and have the students paint in the colors. Students should be trained in advance in painting techniques and especially in how to paint things that will appear in the backdrop, such as sky or trees. Organize the students into small groups with one good leader in each group. Assign a specific task to each group. For example, one group could specialize in clouds, one in sky, one in leaves, and one in bark.

Another way to create a large and effective backdrop is to cover the entire back wall of your stage with canvas paper, which is available by the roll at an art supply store. Rolls can come in very large sizes, so you'll want to get a rough idea of the measurements you want to cover before buying. In general, a roll approximately ten feet high by thirty feet across should cover the backstage wall of most middle school auditoriums. Roll out the paper and paint your backdrop on it. You will need to create holes along the top of the canvas at regular intervals so that it can be hung from the rafters. The effect is like a bathroom shower curtain. Attach grommets to secure the holes. Grommets are metal rings, available in different sizes, which you can click in place with a tool resembling a staple gun. Now, you'll need the school custodians to help hang your backdrop from the rafters.

If your budget is really tight and you cannot afford muslin or canvas paper, remember that it is even possible to create a backdrop by painting on bed sheets!

Create and Arrange the Scenery

Brown "butcher" paper (also known as craft paper) can be very useful in designing scenery. This paper is sold in one-yard rolls, and many art teachers advise purchasing a cutter along with the paper. You can then sit the roll of paper on the cutter, which looks something like a paper towel holder, and easily cut out the size of paper you need.

One art teacher used this approach to create "moody" trees for a production of A Midsummer Night's Dream. She began by rolling the paper out to the required length for a tree trunk. Then, she added to the left and right sides until she got the width she wanted. After cutting out the shape of the tree, she saved excess brown paper from the cutting remains, crumpled it up, and glued it together. The crumpling creates a play with light so the material looks like tree bark. She used this crumpled material for the trunk and branches, and dabbed over it using different shades of brown to get the tone she wanted. (An art teacher can even add gloss to certain parts of the tree, but this should be done when there are no students around, since the smell is strong and could make a child ill.) The way the crumpled material reflected light gave the trees the exotic and mysterious quality she needed for A Midsummer Night's Dream.

Establish Different Levels of Height

You can suggest different levels of height by putting some scenery on rolling scaffolding and rolling ladders, which can be easily purchased in a Home Depot type of store. Now you can create bigger and taller scenery that can be moved around, as opposed to stationary scenery, which may have trouble standing on its own if it is too large or too tall. For example, one art teacher needed a large palm tree for the scene in *Guys and Dolls* set in Havana, Cuba. She designed her tree so that it was supported by a rolling ladder from behind. This way, she was able to come up with something on a large scale without having to construct her palm tree from scratch.

Safety Issues

All scenery should be constructed with safety in mind. Let's talk first about stage flats (scenery mounted on flat, moveable frames). Every flat item used onstage as scenery should have a jack or other means of support behind it. Sometimes directors will even add an additional stage weight, such as a sandbag, on top of the jack. If you don't take these precautions, students may lean against the flat and fall.

Make sure any platforms that students will stand on have adequate support underneath, so no one falls through the flooring. Any platform or level higher than two or three feet from the ground must have railings to prevent the possibility of students falling off during rehearsals or performances.

Sometimes a director will try to add a different texture to the floor, perhaps to make it look like cement. Be aware of what materials are being used to create that look as well as the physical effects they could have on students who may be on their hands and knees either preparing for the show or acting in the show. You don't want to be responsible for sore hands and knees! Also be aware that any water onstage can create a very slippery floor surface.

Know and follow your school's fire regulations at all times, and watch what materials you use near the theatre lights. For example, avoid using plastic near the stage lights, as these lights can become extremely hot.

The students' role in set design and scenery preparation should involve preparing and hanging scenery at their own height level. Students should not climb ladders and should not be involved with anything electrical, including plugging in any connections or handling any wires. Students should not be involved in any kind of carpentry work unless they are part of an industrial arts class and supervised by a licensed industrial arts teacher.

When you paint your backdrop, have students work with either water-based or latex-based paint. Latex is considered good because it dries quickly and is generally safer. Try not to use anything stronger than acrylic paint. You should definitely avoid spray paint; it can contain toxic chemicals. One art teacher recalls painting a school backdrop with spray paint when she was a fifth grader. After an afternoon of working with this paint, she became sick and was confined to bed for several days. Another type of paint that can cause problems is glossy paint. Avoid working with it when students are around. Glossy paint gives off a strong smell and can make some students ill.

These and other safety considerations are summarized in the safety guidelines that can be found in figure 7.1 in chapter 7.

Develop a Good Relationship with Your School Custodians
It is extremely important that you obtain the help and goodwill of your school's custodial staff. It is especially essential that the art teachers and custodians work hand-in-hand. A good working relationship with the custodians is critical to your show's success. As you begin to plan the musical, let your principal know that you would like to meet with the head custodian. At the meeting, explain your plans for the show, talk about the things you'll need help with, and give this person an idea of your timeline.

The head custodian can help you secure the necessary permits for using the auditorium for the performances of your musical. He or she can then assign individual members of the custodial staff to assist you. Do not approach custodians in the middle of their shift to ask for immediate help hanging scenery. Even if they are willing to help you out at a moment's notice, they could get in trouble for not completing whatever assignment they were supposed to be doing. Always plan ahead and get the head custodian's approval in advance.

MAKEUP TIPS

A Broadway makeup artist once told me, "Everyone wants to be beautiful, even if they are playing a monster! Even in *Cats*, they all want to be beautifully done." Applying makeup requires undivided attention. Since you must focus your attention on many aspects of the production, makeup is not something you should be personally involved with. Find a colleague or parent volunteer who is willing to take charge of makeup activities and recruit interested students (either from your school or perhaps from a nearby high school) to serve as makeup assistants. If you happen to have a parent who works in the makeup business, see if you can recruit that parent to help out. This person's expertise will be invaluable, and he or she may be able to help you get some free supplies. Offer to give the company free advertising and a thank-you acknowledgment in the printed program.

A minimalist approach to makeup can bring out the beauty in your middle school students and will save you money and aggravation. Simply put, use makeup only when and where you need it.

Middle school students generally have beautiful skin so foundation is not necessary. Focus on defining the students' faces by accentuating their eyebrows, eyelashes, and lips. The eyes and mouth are the most expressive parts of the face and need to be clearly seen by the audience. Brush eyebrows upward to create more space between the lash and the brow. Define the eyebrows with pencil, shadow, or liquid liner. Then, curl the lash and apply a little mascara. These techniques will make students' eyes appear larger onstage.

Use a lip pencil to bring out the lips. You can apply lip gloss or lipstick over that if necessary. Keep in mind that if the lip color you are using is too close to a student's skin color, the lips will not show up onstage. Highlight the features of Caucasian students with darker colors so that they stand out against white skin. Highlight the features of darker-skinned students with somewhat lighter colors. For example, you might use a cream-colored pencil on a darker-skinned student, as opposed to brown or black on a light-skinned student. Now, your students' faces are ready for the stage!

Today's theatre celebrates diversity of skin color. The growing acceptance of nontraditional casting has made it possible for white actors and actresses to portray black characters and black actors to portray white characters without the actors drastically altering their skin color for the performance. Changing a student performer's skin color by more than two tones in either direction should always be avoided unless the student will be portraying an alien creature such as a "blue man," or a green-faced plant in *Little Shop of Horrors*.

COSTUMES AND PROPS

In an ideal world, every school would be able to order beautiful costumes perfectly and specifically suited for the musical being produced and the children who will wear them. This is hardly ever the case in real life. The process of finding appropriate costumes and props requires creativity, networking, and some footwork. At the beginning of the year, once you have decided which musical you will produce, let everyone in the school community know what kinds of costumes and props you will need and ask for their help in finding or donating these items.

Recruit several parents to be in charge of helping with costumes, and ask them to canvass Salvation Army and other thrift stores. See if these stores will temporarily donate the items you need for the show, and let them know that you will return the items promptly following the performances. If the stores are not willing to lend you the items, see if your school will allow you to buy them (the prices should be reasonable at these stores).

Next, follow the same procedure with area department stores. Perhaps they would be willing to donate some inexpensive items in return for a promotional advertisement in your printed program. Also, these stores may have irregular or imperfect merchandise they were planning to discard. You may be able to get these items at no charge.

Many corporations that do window dressing for the holidays have large prop departments. Contact them and explain that you are a public school teacher in charge of producing a musical. Ask if they have any props they could donate to the school for your production. You should also contact amateur, local, and regional theatrical companies in your area. They might be willing to lend some costumes and props to your school. Finally, try to establish a network with other schools in your area for the purposes of sharing costumes, props, and scenery items as needed. This promotes greater interschool cooperation and benefits everyone.

I usually had the students in my chorus wear white shirts/blouses and dark pants/skirts. This generic outfit can then be accessorized to suit the theme of the musical. For example, they can wear sailor hats for *South Pacific*, cowboy hats for *Oklahoma*, sunglasses for *Grease*, and baseball caps for *Damn Yankees*. Party stores and catalogs can be a wonderful resource for reasonably priced accessories or for simple outfits.

Finding Additional Materials on a Tight Budget

DonorsChoose is an organization designed to match potential donors with school projects that need financing. Teachers submit a description of the project (for example, painting the backdrop for a musical) and list the resources needed along with the estimated cost. The organization then posts the information on their website where donors can read about the different proposals and fund a project that they are interested in. Most proposals that are funded come from schools in low-income communities. For more information, go to their website: www.donorschoose.org.

LIGHTING

The most important thing to remember about lighting for a school musical is that the audience should be able to see every student who is performing onstage. Since every actor must be seen, directors may have to adjust their blocking plans to conform to the capabilities of the school's lighting system. Your school may already have an audio-visual person who handles assemblies and special events. If not, find a colleague with some knowledge and interest who is willing to handle the lighting for the musical. If all else fails, see if you can hire the audio-visual person from a nearby high school or else a responsible high school student who has had experience in his or her school's lighting crew.

The director of lighting should recruit students from your school to serve on a lighting crew. Students working on the lighting crew should be given specific assignments depending on their age and experience. Younger, less experienced students can assist the older, more experienced students. Some schools train sixth-grade crew members to follow the script and cue the seventh and eighth graders, who actually operate the lights. When these sixth graders become seventh and eighth graders, it will then be their turn to run the lights.

If your auditorium has an older lighting system, you may have a combination of proscenium lights controlled by dimmers, one or two "follow" spot lights that are operated from an overhead lighting booth, and maybe a few smaller, portable spotlights that can be operated from the audience. The proscenium lights can usually illuminate the stage in several basic colors. The junior high school where I worked could light the stage in red, yellow, and blue.

Before you get started, check to make sure that all the bulbs are in working order. To replace bulbs, you may need to crank down the rows of lights and then crank them up again when you're done.

The follow spotlights literally follow a singer/actor around the stage with either white light or a variety of colors. There is no way to blend the colors; you have to use one at a time. Follow spotlights are approximately four and a half feet tall by three and a half feet long and are mounted on wheels. Follow spots can be slightly bulky (one teacher described them as "little cannons") and it can require some practice to operate them smoothly. You will need to train the students assigned to each follow spot to hold the light steadily. Assign individual crew members to follow specific lead characters.

Some schools may also have a few smaller, portable spotlights that can be operated from the audience. Each of these smaller lights can be operated by a single student. Assign a younger "apprentice" to help and learn from this student.

Prior to the first full rehearsal, it is extremely important that the lighting crew advisor go over the script and the cues with all the members of the crew and make sure everyone writes the cues into their scripts. The advisor should also spend at least one full technical rehearsal in the lighting booth, talking about the cues and showing the students what needs to be done and how to do it. One crew member should be assigned to call out the cues as the play progresses. For example, Cue number five might read, "Dimmer #8: 50 percent." When the assigned student calls out "Cue number five," the students in charge of the dimmers will set the proscenium light controls at 50 percent of their capacity.

If your school has a newer lighting system, it will probably be computerized. You will be able to preprogram the lights for different settings using a digital board by simply entering all the necessary information into the system. For example, you can program light number one for a single speaker, number two for the chorus, and number three for the band. Computerized lighting systems can save a great deal of time, and you will need only one student to operate the system.

REMAIN RESOURCEFUL AND ENTHUSIASTIC

While the many details of stage sets, scenery, makeup, costumes, and lighting may seem overwhelming at first glance, it is important to keep in mind that you are not preparing a production for Broadway but for middle school students, their parents, and the community. Getting your students and their audience excited and involved in the show is the most important thing. If some of the materials you end up using are not exactly your first choice, this should have little to no effect on the overall success of your show. Good theatre is all about imagination! Remain excited and enthused about the show, and you and your students are likely to enjoy an inspired performance even with minimal materials.

9

STUDENT, PARENT, AND SCHOOLWIDE INVOLVEMENT IN FUNDRAISING, PUBLICITY, AND PROMOTION

Students, parents, colleagues, school administrators, and community members can be significant sources of help and support for the musical. This chapter describes how specific groups can contribute to achieving a successful show in your community.

ADDITIONAL STUDENT INVOLVEMENT

You already have at your disposal the boundless energy and enthusiasm of all the students who will be involved in the production. In addition, students who work on the school newspaper can be quite helpful in promoting the show.

Once you have selected the musical, see if the newspaper can announce the dates and times of the auditions and performances. Invite reporters from the school newspaper to observe rehearsals, interview members of the cast and crews, and write an article about the show. Encourage the student reporters to take pictures to accompany the article. Finally, offer student reporters free tickets to the performance so they can write an article about it. Give them another opportunity to take pictures directly before or after the performance. For example, the curtain call is a good time to take pictures of the entire cast. Articles in the student newspaper can help to make everyone in the school aware of and excited about the musical and should result in increased student attendance at the performances.

WORKING WITH PARENT VOLUNTEERS

Since many of their children will be in the show, parents are especially motivated to help make the production a success. To get the best results from parent helpers, you need to provide guidelines and parameters for their involvement. Make sure that parent volunteers have clear and specific assignments so that they know exactly what you need them to do.

At the beginning of the year, send a letter to all parents announcing the show as well as the dates, times, and locations of auditions. Also, this letter should announce any specific items you may need in the areas of scenery, costumes, or props. Provide a tear-off section at the bottom of the letter where parents can indicate an area they would like to help with. For example, you might give parents the option to help out with any of the following: costumes, props, makeup, ticket sales, backstage patrol, the cast party, promotion, or advertising. Within two weeks of receiving the tear-offs, contact the prospective parent volunteers to learn more about their skills and talents. Now you will have enough information to give them specific and appropriate assignments.

If you don't get enough parent volunteers, try to recruit interested colleagues, responsible students from your school, or interested students from a nearby high school. You can then pair some of the students and colleagues with those parents who did volunteer. For example, your advertising committee might include a combination of students, a parent, and another teacher.

INVOLVE YOUR COLLEAGUES AND YOUR PRINCIPAL

Cultivating good relations with all your colleagues and with your principal can be of tremendous benefit. If you make every effort to support your colleagues' events and projects, they will in turn help you. One music teacher described how she serves on the school's science fair committee every year and supports the athletic events by attending and even occasionally volunteering for locker room patrol during a game. In return, she has always received support and cooperation from her peers. Her colleagues cooperate when she needs to pull students for rehearsals, and they even volunteer to help backstage on the nights of the show.

The same spirit applies to relations with your principal. Principals appreciate teachers who work cooperatively with their colleagues and demonstrate an interest in schoolwide events. Some music teachers offer cameo roles to their principal and several popular teachers. This can be a successful strategy for giving the principal and your other colleagues a personal interest in the show. It is also a great experience for the students who will actually work side by side with their principal and other teachers. For example, one music teacher included her principal and his family in a production of *Guys and Dolls*. They appeared briefly in the background of a scene set in Times Square, where they walked around, pointing at the buildings and the skyline. In *Fiddler on the Roof*, the same principal along with another faculty member appeared as patrons seated in the tavern during the scene featuring the song "To Life."

FUNDRAISING

If you are producing a musical for the first time, chances are you will not have much of a budget to work with. You'll need to let your principal know the anticipated costs for the production, which must include licensing and royalty fees. If your school does not have a budget for musicals, the next step will be to develop a plan for raising money for this and future productions. Speak with your principal about the possibility of charging ticket prices that all the students and their families will be able to afford. Ask each student involved in the show to sell tickets to friends and neighbors. Set a goal of ten tickets per student, allowing them to return any tickets they were unable to sell.

Start to build a steady source of additional financial support for your musicals by developing good relationships with local businesses. Offer them the opportunity to advertise in your show's printed program. Set reasonable fees for options, such as a business card (four to six on a page), a half-page, or a full-page display. If you are not sure what to charge, contact nearby schools or local community theatre groups and ask what they charge. Figure 9.1 contains a letter that you can adapt and use to solicit advertisements from local businesses. Figure 9.2 shows some sample advertisements.

Remember to approach big businesses such as chain supermarkets early in January for a spring performance. They will need some lead time in order to obtain approval from their corporate office. One middle school in upper New York State became so adept at soliciting advertisements that their printed program grew to the size of a local phone directory!

All of this is much too time-consuming for you to handle alone. Delegate this operation to a group of parent volunteers. You will also need the help of school personnel to print a nice-looking program. After the show is over, write a thank-you note to each of the patrons. Drop off copies of the program to those local businesses

Name and Address of Your School
(school letterhead)

Dear Patron:

_____ Middle School is proud to announce that our annual musical production for this year is _____. The performance will be on [day of the week, month, day, and year] at 7:30 PM and [day of the week, month, day, and year] at 2:00 PM. It has been a community tradition for our local businesses to support our productions by choosing to advertise in our program.

We are offering the following space in the patrons' portion of our program:

Business Card (four business cards to a page)	$ 5
Half-Page Advertisement (two patrons to a page)	$10
Full-Page Advertisement (one patron to a page)	$15

We hope you will join our community in wishing success and best wishes to a very hardworking cast and crew. Messages should be written below and sent to me by [day of the week, month, day, and year]. Thank you in advance for your interest and cooperation. Please call with any questions or concerns.

Sincerely,

Name of Director

_____

Please make checks payable to [name of your school] and send to:

Name of Your School
Att: Name of Director
Address of School

Name of Business _____

Please check one of the following:

Business Card	$ 5 _____	(please attach business card)
*Half Page	$10 _____	
*Full Page	$15 _____	

*For half-page or full-page advertisements, please write the message as you would like it to appear in the program. Feel free to attach brochure or company logo.

Figure 9.1.   Letter to Local Businesses

Royal Crest Limousine Service

Quality for Less
Proms Our Specialty
7773 Eagle's Nest Circle
Glastonbury, NY 00004

Phone 555-0060

DISTINCTIVE DESIGNS
Phone: 555-555-9999 | Fax 555-555-1919

distinctive@pfdesigns.com

Hello Sunshine! Day Care

Olive Newman-James
Director

111 Route 365N
Plato, NY 00006

Phone: 555.555.6171
Fax: 555.555.0144

Montessori Curriculum

Figure 9.2.   Sample Advertisements

that contributed so that they can see their ads in print. These small gestures can help to generate a good rapport with your patrons and ensure that they continue to contribute in the future. After a few years, many schools find that they actually have to turn away potential advertisers once the program has to finally go to print!

Another way of generating revenue through the printed program is to sell space where parents, teachers, and friends can print messages to cast members. Charge a minimal amount for each of these messages. People enjoy writing the messages, and cast members enjoy reading them. This tradition will become popular, and the money will add up. Figure 9.3 contains a letter that you can adapt and use to solicit messages for your printed program. Figure 9.4 shows some sample messages.

After the success of your first musical production, draw up your budget for next year and meet with your principal. Having just finished the show, you will have an even clearer idea of what your expenses might be for the next time. Do this as quickly as possible while pleasant memories of the musical are still fresh in everyone's mind. It is extremely important that the anticipated expenses for the yearly musical be included in the school budget.

Do not accept the rationale that you can support the musical through fundraising, even if you have managed to raise a lot of money this year! Your school's musical is part of a legitimate unit of study, not an extracurricular activity. The school community has just seen how successful the annual musical can be. Take advantage of the moment and make your case.

PUBLICIZING AND PROMOTING THE SHOW

It is very important to spread the word about your show throughout the local community. Contact the local newspapers and try to get a reporter to attend a rehearsal and to take pictures of the students onstage. Hopefully the article that appears in print will generate interest in the show and will announce the performance

Dear Parents, Relatives, and Friends of Our [name of show] Cast,

You are cordially invited to our annual [name of school] Musical. Tickets are $ [price] and will be going on sale soon.

Once again, we are going to offer you the opportunity to have messages printed in the program to show your support for the cast. Messages will be $ [price] for a third of a page. An example of a message is as follows:

TO THE CAST AND CREW OF
[NAME OF MUSICAL]
BREAK A LEG!
From the Tech Department at [name of your school]

(Please limit your message to 75 letters.)

Messages should be printed below and given to me with a check for $ _____ by [give a deadline for about seven weeks before the performance].

Sincerely,

[Name of Director]
• •

Name of Cast Member: _____

Attach a $ _____ check. Please make checks payable to:
[Name of Your School] Musical

I would like my message to read as follows:

Figure 9.3. Letter to Solicit Messages to Cast and Crew Members

dates, times, location, and ticket prices. Then, send the different local newspapers complimentary tickets to the performance and see if their reporters can write another article about the performance itself.

Do you, your students, other teachers, and parents know anyone who works in radio or television? If so, try to enlist their help in promoting the show. For example, one teacher learned that the

> Andrew
> You're a star now!
> Love from
> Mom, Dad, Shelly, David,
> and Tweety

> Another Show,
> Another
> Successful Year!
> Congratulations!
> The Glastonbury
> P.T.A.

> To everyone in the chorus,
>
> This year has been the most fun ever!
>
> Love you all!
>
> Amy, Denise, and Sharon

Figure 9.4. Sample Messages to Cast and Crew Members

father of one of her students worked as a DJ for a local radio station. That year, the radio station not only announced details of the upcoming performance but also broadcast excerpts of some of the songs sung by the students!

Don't forget to notify your fellow music teachers in nearby schools about the performance. Pay special attention to the elementary schools that feed into your school. Consider inviting these schools to a daytime performance of the musical. If the show seems too long for an elementary child's attention span, perform selected scenes. This can generate interest in your program and can give your students a chance to practice their performance in front of a live audience, prior to opening night.

Are there any senior citizen residences or community centers in your area? If so, consider scheduling a free morning or afternoon performance specifically for senior citizens. Contact the residences or centers and invite them to bring their members to the performance. If this is not feasible, offer senior citizens free admission to your regularly scheduled performances. Seniors usually have a great time at these events and will appreciate the work you are doing. Remember that these citizens vote on school tax bills! You can also arrange to visit an area senior center, library, or other public area to perform either an abbreviated version of your show, or to simply present selected excerpts.

In either case, you'll need to find a way to help the audience understand the flow of the story, since the shortened presentations will likely omit sections of dialogue and some of the musical numbers. I suggest having one or two student narrators create and deliver a verbal presentation that will tie everything together for the audience. This verbal presentation can be read or memorized. Now the audience members will feel that they have experienced the full show. This approach also allows your narrators, who may not be part of the actual cast of the show, to be featured in an important role. Work with the narrators so that they feel confident. Help them to clearly enunciate their words, speak at a moderate speed, and project their voices.

The ideas in this chapter will help you to get students, parents, colleagues, administrators, and members of the community excited and involved in helping to make the musical a success. Remember that it is impossible for you to do everything yourself. Take advantage of these people's willingness to assist you. Give specific assignments and guidance. After the first year or two, you will have a functioning routine in place that includes recruiting volunteers, delegating assignments, and promoting your show within the school and community.

CREATE AN ORIGINAL MUSICAL

While it is always exciting to produce a well-known musical, some teachers also enjoy helping their students to create and present original musicals. In this chapter, we'll talk about several approaches you can use. The first is what I call the modified Sing approach. The second features the music teacher as composer and lyricist. The third involves students creating the lyrics and the teacher writing the music. The fourth has students creating both the lyrics and some of the music, under the teacher's guidance.

THE MODIFIED SING APPROACH

Some high schools have an annual "Sing" where each grade creates and presents its own musical production. A sing is considered an after-school activity and often has no direct connection to the school's music program. Each grade's show competes against the other grades to be named the winning Sing. All the shows are written, performed, and produced by students with assistance from a faculty advisor. Generally, the students in each grade select a theme, build the storyline around it, and create a script. A committee of students chooses popular, folk, or Broadway melodies, and a lyric committee rewrites the text to these songs in order to suit the plot. You can adapt the concept behind Sing to the middle school level and use it as a way to help students create a musical.

Eliminate the element of competition by having only one schoolwide production instead of a production for each grade level. Involve everyone in the school who would normally be part of a school musical. Ask your colleagues in other subject areas if they would be interested in being part of this project. Since middle school students are not quite as ready to work on their own as high school students might be, incorporate your students' creative work into music and other subject-area classes, particularly language arts. Now you and your colleagues can supervise the students at work in a structured setting while providing direction and guidance.

THE MUSIC TEACHER AS COMPOSER/LYRICIST

Many music teachers are capable of writing terrific shows. This approach can work well if you have the time and the talent to write a musical and if you enjoy the work involved. Your students will be excited to perform in a musical written by their teacher. This approach does not allow for much creativity on the students' part in terms of creating a musical, since you have already written the show for them. However, there may be other aspects of the musical, such as planning and designing the scenery or inventing original choreography, where you can involve the students as creative partners.

STUDENTS CREATE LYRICS/TEACHER WRITES THE MUSIC

Another approach to creating an original musical is to have your students create the song lyrics while you compose the music. Let your students give you suggestions for a topic, theme, or story and involve everyone in the final decision.

One middle school music teacher described how she formed a committee of students and teachers including the language arts faculty. The committee played an important role in creating the musical. Members of the committee visited the school's language arts and music classrooms. They asked students in those classes for their ideas about what structure and form the show should take. For example, should the show be a revue or would it have a clear story line? What would the topic or theme of the show be? In different years, students in that school came up with topics for the musical such as teen concerns, current events, and the neighborhood. The students wrote the script, decided where the songs should occur, and created the song lyrics in their language arts classes. The music teacher then set those lyrics to music to be performed as solos, duets, or full ensemble. This sort of approach establishes a nice working partnership between teachers and students.

STUDENTS CREATE THE LYRICS AND MUSIC

In this approach, the students are full participants in the creative process. They write the lyrics and you can help them compose some of the music. You can find sample lesson plans focused on helping students try their hand at composing in *Strategies for Teaching Middle-Level General Music* (Hinckley and Shull, 1996). Work with your entire class and visualize yourself as a partner, coach, and mentor. For example, if you and your students are working on setting the lyrics of a particular song to music, you might suggest possible choices for the song's melody and harmony. Then let the students make a group decision. Play the results back on the piano or through a tape recorder. Let the students critique what they wrote so far. They can determine whether they will keep it or whether they want to revise it some more.

Helping your students compose some of the music to the show

is by far the most challenging of the four approaches to creating original musicals that we have discussed. Because this process will be time-consuming, you should plan to start working on writing the musical in the early fall so you are ready to cast the show in January. Be sure that your students are mature and interested enough to handle the work and to commit their energies to this project. Also, encourage and incorporate the work of students who have outstanding musical ability. For example, a middle school teacher told me that, one year, a young man in her class played several melodies on the piano for her that he had composed by ear. With his permission, the teacher incorporated those melodies into the show. In addition, several of her general music classes developed rhythm patterns to accompany some of the songs that he had written.

AN APPROACH WORTH EXPLORING

Creating original musicals can provide a perfect opportunity to work with students and teachers in other subject areas. Involving your students as playwrights, lyricists, and, in some cases, composers, brings the essence of the national standards to life in your classroom. Activities such as these will harness the creative energies of your students and give them incredible pride in their work. In addition, this can be a great challenge and source of joy for the music teacher who loves creating and composing. If working on original musicals appeals to you, and you are comfortable working collaboratively with your students, consider giving it a try.

COPYRIGHT CONSIDERATIONS

If you think you and your students' work is valuable beyond the school, you should consider getting it copyrighted so the creators of the work are protected. While it is true that original work in the performing arts is, in theory, automatically protected from the date of creation, it is still prudent to register for and receive a certificate of copyright for your work. This establishes a public record of your copyright claim and gives you the exclusive right to reproduce the work, to prepare derivative works, to distribute copies, or to perform or display the work publicly.

If you or your students are considering rewriting lyrics to songs that you intend to perform, make sure you request and receive permission from the rights holder. If the song you want to use happens to be in the public domain, you are free to do as you please. Traditional folk songs are generally considered public domain.

You may want to consider integrating a lesson or two about creativity and copyright into the curriculum of the unit of study. The language arts and music teachers can talk to the students about what it means to be part of the creative community. Students can learn how to protect their own creative work and how to respect and protect other creative people's rights. MENC has written sample lessons dealing with this subject. You can find those lesson plans by accessing MENC's copyright center at www.menc.org. and clicking on Creativity in the Classroom.

For more information about copyright issues, visit MENC's copyright center at www.menc.org or the United States Copyright Office at www.loc.copyright.

11

ASSESS THE UNIT OF STUDY

This chapter helps you create formative and summative assessment activities you can use to demonstrate what your students learned, suggests ways to evaluate the success of your whole unit of study, and explains how your assessment process can be a valuable tool for advocacy.

ASSESSING STUDENT ACHIEVEMENT

In addition to involving the teachers in creating assessment activities, whenever possible, try to involve the students in designing some of the assessments. This will give your students a clearer understanding of what they will be learning, and of how to demonstrate what they have learned. Include students who will be participating in the production as well as students whose classroom work will involve the musical as a focus of learning.

Assessments can be given at any point during the project, or at the end of the unit. For example, the choral teacher might have students listen to and critique a recording of their singing at any time during the unit of study to identify areas of strength as well as things that need improvement. The art teacher might require students to critique their work on the scenery midway through the unit of study. These types of activities are called *formative assess-*

ments since the students are still developing their skills and the unit is not yet over. The same critiques conducted at the project's completion would be considered *summative assessments* because you are assessing the students' final work in that unit of study. If you assign your students to keep a running journal as they move through the unit of study, this could be considered a formative assessment. A reaction paper assigned to students at the conclusion of the unit of study would be a summative assessment.

It is useful to design some formative and some summative assessments for your project so that you and your colleagues can examine the effectiveness of the curriculum and teaching at various points along the way. Try to stagger these activities. Students shouldn't have too many assessments scheduled on the same day.

SAMPLE OBJECTIVES AND ASSESSMENTS FOR *THE KING AND I*

In chapter 2 we talked about designing a hypothetical unit of study based on *The King and I* and included sample objectives and methods of assessment in vocal and instrumental music, visual art, dance, theatre arts, language arts, and social studies. For easy reference, we linked each objective and method of assessment to one of the national standards for the subject area. Tables 11.1 through 11.7 summarize that information.

Table 11.1. Vocal Music Assessment

Objective	Content Standard	Method of Assessment
1. Students will perform selected songs from *The King and I* accurately with good posture and breath control.	#1. Singing, alone and with others, a varied repertoire of music.	Teacher evaluates individual and small group performances of the repertoire in class.
2. Students will perform selected songs from *The King and I* observing the appropriate dynamic and tempo markings.	#1. Singing, alone and with others, a varied repertoire of music.	Teacher evaluates individual and small group performances of the repertoire in class.
3. Students will listen to and critique their recorded performance using teacher- and student-developed criteria.	#7. Evaluating music and music performances.	Teacher evaluates student critiques based on use of predetermined criteria.
4. Students will listen to a professional cast recording of *The King and I*, identifying the basic meter, rhythm, and mode of the selections they are learning.	#6. Listening to, analyzing, and describing music.	Teacher evaluates student responses during group listening and discussion.

Table II.2.   Instrumental Music Assessment

Objective	Content Standard	Method of Assessment
I. Students will perform selections from the score of *The King and I* as part of an ensemble, accurately and independently, with good posture, good playing position and good breath, bow, or stick control.	#2. Performing on instruments, alone and with others, a varied repertoire of music.	Teacher evaluates individual and small group performances of the repertoire in class.
2. Students will perform selections from *The King and I* observing the appropriate articulation, dynamic, and tempo markings.	#2. Performing on instruments, alone and with others, a varied repertoire of music.	Teacher evaluates individual and small group performances of the repertoire in class.
3. Students will listen to and critique their recorded performance using teacher- and student-developed criteria.	#7. Evaluating music and music performances.	Teacher will evaluate student critiques based on use of predetermined criteria.
4. Students will listen to a professional cast recording of *The King and I*, identifying the basic meter, rhythm, and mode of the selections they are learning.	#6. Listening to, analyzing, and describing music.	Teacher evaluates student responses during group listening and discussion.

Table 11.3.   Visual Art Assessment

Objective	Content Standard	Method of Assessment
1. Students will demonstrate the ability to choose specific media, techniques and processes that will successfully communicate the theme of the musical.	#1. Understanding and applying media, techniques, and processes.	Teacher evaluates individual students' progress.
2. Students will select subjects for the scenery that reflect the theme of Southeast Asian history and culture.	#3. Choosing and evaluating a range of subject matter, symbols, and ideas.	Teacher evaluates students' selected subjects for relevance to the project's theme. Students explain their choice of subject in a brief written statement.
3. Students will create scenery and stage sets working with paint, paper, and fabrics.	#1. Understanding and applying media, techniques, and processes.	Teacher observes and evaluates each student's work in terms of both process and product.
4. Students will reflect on and critique their own work and the work of their peers, both verbally and in writing, using teacher- and student-developed criteria.	#5. Reflecting upon and assessing the characteristics and merits of their work and the work of others.	Teacher observes students during class discussions and group critiques. Teacher evaluates students' written responses.

Table 11.4.   Dance Assessment

Objective	Content Standard	Method of Assessment
1. Students will demonstrate the ability to remember and perform extended movement sequences to music.	#1. Identifying and demonstrating movement elements and skills in performing dance.	Teacher and students evaluate videotapes or DVDs of student rehearsals at successive intervals during the semester.
2. Students will demonstrate rhythmic acuity.	#1. Identifying and demonstrating movement elements and skills in performing dance.	Teacher observes students' rhythmic acuity at successive intervals during the semester.
3. Students will use improvisation to generate movement for choreography.	#2. Understanding choreographic principles, processes, and structures.	Teacher observes students' degree of participation in improvisation exercises.

Table 11.5.   Theatre Arts Assessment

Objective	Content Standard	Method of Assessment
1. Students will analyze the plot of The King and I in order to explain the motivation behind the characters' actions and invent character behaviors, communicating their findings through performance exercises and written reflections.	#2. Acting by developing basic acting skills to portray characters who interact in improvised and scripted scenes.	Teacher monitors student performance exercises and written reflections.
2. Students will demonstrate acting skills, including eye contact, concentration, vocal projection, and diction.	#2. Acting by developing basic acting skills to portray characters who interact in improvised and scripted scenes.	Teacher observes and evaluates individual students' initial skill level and subsequent growth.
3. Students will work in small groups to rehearse scripted scenes, demonstrating social, group, and consensus skills.	#4. Directing by organizing rehearsals for improvised and scripted scenes.	Teacher observes how students work together and evaluates performance.

Table 11.6.   Language Arts Assessment

Objective	Content Standard	Method of Assessment
1. Students will locate past performance reviews of *The King and I* using the *New York Times* Index and other databases recommended by the teacher. Students will read and bring copies of these reviews to class.	#8. Students use a variety of technological and information resources to gather and synthesize information and to create and communicate knowledge.	Teacher collects the printed performance reviews and verifies that they came from the recommended sources. Students complete a worksheet requiring them to analyze the material in the printed review.
2. Through written essays, students will compare and contrast the libretto of *The King and I* with the book that inspired it, *Anna and the King of Siam*. They will explain how using different literary genres (libretto and memoir) can affect the presentation of a story.	#2. Students read a wide range of literature from many periods in many genres to build an understanding of the many dimensions (e.g., philosophical, ethical, aesthetic) of human experience.	Teacher evaluates student essays.
3. Students will read and discuss the libretto of *The King and I* and the book *Anna and the King of Siam*. They will locate examples of Siamese attitudes toward women and Anna's attitudes toward the women of the King's harem as expressed in these two literary works.	#1. Students read a wide range of print and nonprint texts to build an understanding of texts, of themselves, and of the cultures of the United States and the world.	Teacher evaluates student responses during class discussion.

Table 11.7. Social Studies Assessment

Objective	Content Standard	Method of Assessment
1. Students will demonstrate the ability to locate Thailand on a world map and to locate and identify neighboring countries (e.g., Vietnam).	#3. Study of people, places, and environments.	Teacher asks additional questions designed to measure students' understanding of Thailand's location relative to other countries and continents.
2. Through participation in group oral presentations and written essays, students will demonstrate a basic knowledge of the history and culture of Thailand.	#1. Study of culture and cultural diversity. #2. Time, continuity, and change.	Teacher evaluates group oral presentations and written essays.
3. Students will develop questions designed to compare and contrast selected elements of British colonial culture, customs, and attitudes with those of the people of Southeast Asia.	#1. Study of culture and cultural diversity.	Teacher evaluates students' written questions.

SELECT AN ASSESSMENT ACTIVITY

In order to assess student achievement, you and your colleagues should first review the objectives you designed for each subject area in your unit of study. For each objective, decide on the method of assessment you want to use to measure whether or not students have achieved that objective. You will find it easier to measure student success if your objectives involve students actively doing something or producing something. If your objectives are not specific or active enough, it will be more difficult if not impossible to measure student accomplishment.

Devise rubrics that will help you rate each student's performance quickly and objectively. This chapter provides examples of simple grids, Likert-type scales, and student worksheets that you can use and adapt to your needs. For example, the simple grids illustrated in this chapter are suggested templates. The ratings go from the highest to the lowest (top to bottom). Feel free to incorporate whatever scoring system you prefer on the left side of the grid. For example, you can use A, B, C, D, F or 1, 2, 3, 4, 5 or exemplary, proficient, developing, needs work, below standard.

Let's focus on one of the suggested objectives and methods of assessment for each subject area in our hypothetical unit of study. For each of these, we'll include a sample rubric and describe how a possible assessment activity might play out in the classroom.

Vocal Music

The first objective for Vocal Music in our sample unit of study states: students will perform selected songs from *The King and I* accurately with good posture and breath control. This objective is clear and easy to measure; the students can either do these things or they can't. Our suggested method of assessment was for the teacher to evaluate individual and small group performances of the repertoire in class. This assessment activity requires that students apply some basic concepts and skills they have been working on all year to the specific vocal parts they are learning for the musical.

Try using this activity, or one like it, as part of your choral midterm exam. It will give your students some extra motivation to practice and perfect their parts well before the actual performance of the musical. I used to tell my students, "This is what music students at Juilliard or Peabody have to do and, since you are a talented group of singers, I'm going to expect the same thing from you." Table 11.8 shows a sample rubric grid you can use for this activity.

You can even ask each student in the class to evaluate his or her peers as they perform, using copies of the same rubric. If your students can handle it, this additional assignment will give them

Table II.8.   Sample Rubric for Vocal Music

Name of Presenter(s): _____

Name of Song: _____

Objective: Students will perform selected songs from *The King and I* accurately with good posture and breath control.

Criteria

Accuracy	Posture	Breath Control
Demonstrates accurate pitches and rhythms all of the time.	Demonstrates good singing posture all of the time.	Demonstrates good breath control all of the time.
Demonstrates accurate pitches and rhythms most of the time.	Demonstrates good singing posture most of the time.	Demonstrates good breath control most of the time.
Demonstrates accurate pitches and rhythms some of the time	Demonstrates good singing posture some of the time.	Demonstrates good breath control some of the time.
Demonstrates inaccurate pitches and rhythms most of the time.	Demonstrates poor singing posture most of the time.	Demonstrates poor breath control most of the time.
Demonstrates inaccurate pitches and rhythms all of the time.	Demonstrates poor singing posture all of the time.	Demonstrates poor breath control all of the time.

practice in critical listening and keep them constructively occupied while you are busy evaluating everyone's singing. Make sure the students put their names on the rubric as the evaluators and include the name(s) of the student(s) they are evaluating. At the end of the class period, the students can hand their completed rubrics in to you. You might find it interesting to compare your students' evaluations of their peers with your own. Keep the students' actual written evaluations of their peers confidential. However, you can and should share the general results and suggestions for improvement with the student performers when you hand back your completed rubric form to them.

I want to emphasize that we are evaluating students' singing ability by having them *sing*. It would be inappropriate to assess students' singing skills by giving them a paper and pencil test about the song. That would be an assessment activity requiring different skills and a different mode of learning than those your students were working on. Always be sure to assess student achievement using the same modality of instruction described in your objective.

Step-by-Step Outline of Activity

Objective: Students will perform selected songs from *The King and I* accurately with good posture and breath control.

Method of assessment: Teacher and students evaluate individual and small group performances of the songs in class.

Scoring system: Simple rubric grid (see table 11.8).

Procedures:

1. Have individual or small groups of students sing a portion of the song for you while you rate each performance using the rubric sheet.

2. Give each student in the class the opportunity to evaluate his or her peers as they perform using copies of the same rubric. (This additional assignment will give them practice in critical listening and keep them constructively occupied while you are busy evaluating everyone's singing.)

3. Make sure the students put their names on the rubric as the evaluators and include the name(s) of the student(s) they are evaluating.

4. Have the students hand their completed rubrics in to you at the end of the class period.

5. Keep the students' actual written evaluations of their peers confidential. However, you can and should share the general results and suggestions for improvement with the student performers when you hand back your completed rubric form to them. (You might find it interesting to compare your students' evaluations of their peers with your own.)

Instrumental Music

Whether you are using your regular band class or working with a small rhythm ensemble, you can still benefit from the objectives and methods of assessment described in our table. Our second objective for instrumental music states: students will perform selections from *The King and I* observing the appropriate articulation, dynamic, and tempo markings. You can use the approach we just outlined for vocal music. Your students will simply be playing instruments rather than singing. Table 11.9 is a sample rubric you can use.

Step-by-Step Outline of Activity

Objective: Students will perform selections from *The King and I* observing the appropriate articulation, dynamic, and tempo markings.

Method of assessment: Teacher and students evaluate individual and small group performances of the selections in class.

Scoring system: Simple rubric grid (see table 11.9).

Procedures:

1. Have individual or small groups of students play a portion of the selection for you while you rate each performance using the rubric sheet.
2. Give each student in the class the opportunity to evaluate his or her peers as they perform using copies of the same rubric. (This additional assignment will give them practice in critical listening and keep them constructively occupied while you are busy evaluating everyone's playing.)
3. Make sure the students put their names on the rubric as the evaluators and include the name(s) of the student(s) they are evaluating.
4. Have the students hand their completed rubrics in to you at the end of the class period.
5. Keep the students' actual written evaluations of their peers

Table 11.9.   Sample Rubric for Instrumental Music

Name of Presenter(s): _____

Musical Selection: _____

Objective: Students will perform selections from *The King and I* observing the appropriate articulation, dynamic, and tempo markings.

Criteria

Articulation	Dynamics	Tempo
Observes the appropriate articulation all of the time.	Observes the appropriate dynamic markings all of the time.	Observes the appropriate tempo markings all of the time.
Observes the appropriate articulation most of the time.	Observes the appropriate dynamic markings most of the time.	Observes the appropriate tempo markings most of the time.
Observes the appropriate articulation some of the time.	Observes the appropriate dynamic markings some of the time.	Observes the appropriate tempo markings some of the time.
Observes the appropriate articulation infrequently.	Observes the appropriate dynamic markings infrequently.	Observes the appropriate tempo markings infrequently.
Does not observe appropriate articulations.	Does not observe appropriate dynamic markings.	Does not observe appropriate tempo markings.

confidential. However, you can and should share the general results and suggestions for improvement with the student performers when you hand back your completed rubric form to them. Compare your students' evaluations of their peers with your own.

Visual Art

Our fourth objective for Visual Art reads: Students will reflect on and critique their own work and the work of their peers, both verbally and in writing, using teacher- and student-developed criteria. You can assess student achievement by observing students during class discussions and group critiques and by evaluating the students' written critiques. Hold these group critiques at various points during the course of the semester and at the conclusion of the project.

In order to create the scenery and backdrop, many art teachers organize their students into small groups and give each group a specific job to do. The following assessment activity is designed to evaluate the progress of those groups. The rubric below can be completed by both students and teacher. The teacher can use it to evaluate each group. The students can use it to evaluate their own group as well as the other groups. It is also helpful to keep anecdotal records on the progress of individual students. You can easily adapt this rubric for that purpose.

Table 11.10 is a sample rubric you can use.

Step-by-Step Outline of Activity

Objective: Students will reflect on and critique their own work and the work of their peers, both verbally and in writing, using teacher- and student-developed criteria.

Method of assessment: Observing students during class discussions and group critiques and evaluating the students' written critiques.

Scoring system: Simple rubric grid (see table 11.10).

Procedures:

1. Take a class period and have everyone move through the scenery and backdrop area as if proceeding through a museum exhibit. Give the students enough rubric forms so they can fill one out for every group including their own.

2. Assemble in one location and talk about the evaluations. Discuss the students' progress and identify areas that still need work, emphasizing the criteria you have all agreed on early in the term.

3. Use the sample rubric (see table 11.10) as a guide for your discussion.

Table 11.10.   Sample Rubric for Visual Art

Name(s) of Student(s) in Group: _____

Objective: Students will reflect on and critique their own work and the work of their peers, both verbally and in writing, using teacher- and student-developed criteria.

Criteria

Cultural Aspects	Organization	Creativity/Originality
Students' work reflects the project's theme in choices of subject, color, shape, and form.	Group demonstrated excellent organization and met all deadlines.	Work demonstrates exceptional creativity and originality.
Students' work reflects the project's theme in at least three of the following: subject, color, shape, or form.	Group demonstrated good organization and met most deadlines.	Work demonstrates substantial creativity and originality.
Students' work reflects the project's theme in at least two of the following: subject, color, shape, or form.	Group demonstrated average organization and met some deadlines.	Work demonstrates some creativity and originality.
Students' work reflects the project's theme in at least one of the following: subject, color, shape, or form.	Group demonstrated below average organization and met only a few deadlines.	Work does not demonstrate noticeable creativity and originality.
Students' work does not appear to reflect the project's theme in any of the following: subject, color, shape, or form.	Group demonstrated poor organization and did not meet deadlines.	Work does not demonstrate creativity and originality.

Dance

Our first objective for Dance reads: Students will demonstrate the ability to remember and perform extended movement sequences to music. In order to assess student achievement, record their performance on videotape or DVD during rehearsals at the beginning, middle, and end of the semester. Then, sit down with your students to view their work. Using the categories of memory, performance, and musicality, discuss the students' progress and identify areas that still need work.

Perhaps your school does not have an established dance program, and your dance corps consists of students from the general student population who want to dance in the show. This videotape/assessment activity does not require specialized training on the teacher's part, and will make the dancers feel important and not left out of the evaluation process altogether. Table 11.11 is a sample rubric that you can use.

Step-by-Step Outline of Activity

Objective: Students will demonstrate the ability to remember and perform extended movement sequences to music.

Method of assessment: Critique of performance videotape or DVD.

Scoring system: Simple rubric grid (see table 11.11).

Procedures:

1. Record your students' performance on videotape or DVD during rehearsals at the beginning, middle, and end of the semester.
2. Sit down with your students to view their work.
3. Discuss the students' progress and identify areas that still need work emphasizing the categories of memory, performance, and musicality.
4. Use the sample rubric (see table 11.11) as a guide for your discussion.

Theatre Arts

In our sample unit of study, the first objective for Theatre Arts states: Students will analyze the plot of *The King and I* in order to

Table 11.11. Sample Rubric for Dance

Names of Dancers: _____

Musical Selection: _____

Objective: Students will demonstrate the ability to remember and perform extended movement sequences to music.

Criteria

Memory	Performance	Musicality
Memory in extended movement sequences is accurate all of the time.	Performs with confidence and seems at ease onstage all of the time.	Physical movements demonstrate awareness of and sensitivity to the music all of the time.
Memory in extended movement sequences is accurate most of the time.	Performs with confidence and seems at ease onstage most of the time.	Physical movements demonstrate awareness of and sensitivity to the music most of the time.
Memory in extended movement sequences is accurate some of the time.	Performs with confidence and seems at ease onstage some of the time.	Physical movements demonstrate awareness of and sensitivity to the music some of the time.
Memory in extended movement sequences is infrequently accurate.	Performs with confidence and seems at ease onstage infrequently.	Physical movements demonstrate awareness of and sensitivity to the music infrequently.
Memory in extended movement sequences is inaccurate most of the time.	Does not perform with confidence and seems ill at ease onstage most of the time.	Physical movements do not demonstrate awareness of and sensitivity to the music.

explain the motivation behind the characters' actions and invent character behaviors, communicating their findings through performance exercises and written reflections. For assessment, we suggested that the teacher monitor these performance exercises and written reflections. Early in the semester, as soon as the students have become familiar with the plot, ask everyone to select a character from the show and to ask themselves questions such as: "What does my character want?" "How does my character behave?" and "How would I convey these things to an audience?" Then, have each student answer these questions as part of a brief, written essay describing their character.

Assign the students to small groups. Let each student portray the character they wrote about. Organize the groups so each has a good mix of characters. For example, you probably won't want to have three Annas and two kings in the same group.

Ask each student in the group to describe the motivation behind their character's actions to the others in the group. Next, direct each group to improvise a short scene involving their characters. Explain to the students that they should be able to communicate the motivation behind their characters' actions to the audience through this exercise. The students in each group can decide whether to keep their characters in the time and place of the play or move them to a different time and place. If the students are having trouble getting started, you can suggest that they first come up with a situation, an opening line, and a closing line.

For each group performance you can ask other students in the class to assume the role of audience and critic. You could have one student represent the audience and another a critic and solicit their comments about the group's performance. Or, you can divide the class so that half the students represent the audience and the other half critics. After each group has performed their scene, have a brief discussion between actors and audience. What did the audience think was the motivation behind the characters' action and behavior? Have the actors explain what they were trying to convey and how they were trying to convey it. If this was not apparent to the audience, have the critics suggest possible ways in which the actors could have made these things clearer.

If you do this activity early in the semester, I would recommend not using a rubric for evaluation. One reason is that the students are only beginning to develop their acting skills. A formal rubric might appear threatening at this point. The teacher can make notes on index cards about which students are doing well and who needs extra help. If you want to return to this activity later in the semester, for example as a midterm assessment, you can use a scale-like rubric similar to the sample in figure 11.1. Both you and your students in the audience can fill out one form for each student who performs. Number 1 would represent the student's efforts as least effective. Number 5 would represent the student's efforts as most effective:

Step-by-Step Outline of Activity

Objective: Students will analyze the plot of *The King and I* in order to explain the motivation behind the characters' actions and invent character behaviors, communicating their findings through performance exercises and written reflections.

Method of assessment: Teacher monitors the performance exercises and written reflections.

Scoring system: Rubric in scale form.

Procedures:

1. Early in the semester, as soon as the students have become familiar with the plot, ask everyone to select a character from

---

Name _____

Student's Character _____

Motivation _____

Behavior _____

1. Student conveyed the motivation behind his/her character's actions:

   1_____ 2_____ 3_____ 4_____ 5_____

2. Student conveyed character's behavior:

   1_____ 2_____ 3_____ 4_____ 5_____

3. Student connected with the audience through eye contact:

   1_____ 2_____ 3_____ 4_____ 5_____

Suggestions for Improvement: _____

Figure 11.1. Sample Rubric for Theatre Arts

the show and to ask themselves questions such as: "What
does my character want?" "How does my character behave?"
and "How would I convey these things to an audience?"

2. Have each student answer these questions as part of a brief,
   written essay describing their chosen character.
3. Assign students to small groups to portray the characters they
   wrote about.
4. Organize the groups so each has a good mix of characters.
   For example, you probably won't want to have three Annas
   and two kings in the same group.
5. Ask each student in the group to describe the motivation behind his or her character's actions to the others in the group.
6. Direct each group to improvise a short scene, communicating the motivation behind their characters' actions to the audience. Emphasize the importance of connecting to the
   audience through eye contact.
7. Ask other students in the class to assume the roles of audience and critic for each group performance. You could have
   one student represent the audience and another a critic and
   solicit their comments about the group's performance. Or
   you can divide the class so that half the students represent
   the audience and the other half critics.
8. After each group has performed their scene, have a brief discussion between actors and audience. What did the audience
   think was the motivation behind the characters' actions and
   behavior? Have the actors explain what they were trying to
   convey and how they were trying to convey it. If this was not
   apparent to the audience, have the critics suggest possible
   ways in which the actors could have made these things
   clearer.
9. Teacher and students in the audience fill out a scale-like rubric (see figure 11.1).

Language Arts

Our first objective for Language Arts states: Students will locate past performance reviews of *The King and I* using the *New York Times* Index and other teacher-recommended databases and will read and bring copies of these reviews to class. Collect the copies of these reviews and verify that they came from the recommended sources.

Here is a useful assessment activity you can use during the next class meeting: Hand the reviews back to the students and have the students exchange papers with their neighbors. Give the students sufficient time to read the reviews silently and to record their responses to the following four questions: (1) "Overall, do you think this was a positive or a negative review?" (2) "What are some things the author says that led to your conclusion?" (3) "If the review was generally positive, were there still things the reviewer did not like about the show? What were they?" (4) "If the review was generally negative, were there still things the reviewer liked about the show? What were they?"

At the end of class, collect the reviews and the completed worksheets. Grade the worksheets as you would grade a quiz. In the case of the sample worksheet provided in figure 11.2, assign 25 points for each question.

This assessment activity engages students in research and requires them to analyze and interpret what they are reading. There is an element of surprise involved in this activity because students are reading a review in class that their neighbor brought in.

Step-by-Step Outline of Activity

Objective: Students will locate past performance reviews of *The King and I* using the *New York Times* Index and other teacher-recommended databases and will read and bring copies of these reviews to class.

Reading and Analyzing a Printed Review of *The King and I*

Name: _____

Date: _____

Class: _____

Title of Review Article: _____

Author of Review Article: _____

Year, Date, and Source of Review Article: _____

1. Overall, do you think this review was positive or negative?

_____

2. What are some things the author says that led to your conclusion?

_____

_____

_____

3. If the review was mostly positive, were there things the author did not like about the show? Yes _____ No _____

If yes, what things didn't the author like?

_____

_____

If the review was mostly negative, were there still things the author liked about the show? Yes_____ No_____

If yes, what things did the author like?

_____

_____

Figure 11.2.   Sample Rubric for Language Arts

Method of assessment: Worksheet.

Scoring system: 100 points; 25 points per question.

Procedures:

1. Have students bring a copy of the review to class.
2. Collect the reviews and make sure that they came from the sources you recommended.
3. Note who has handed in their reviews and who has not.

4. During the next class meeting, hand the reviews back to the students and have the students exchange papers with their neighbor to the right.
5. Give the students sufficient time to read the reviews silently.
6. Have everyone complete the worksheet (see figure 11.2).
7. Collect the reviews and the completed worksheets.
8. Grade the worksheets as you would grade a quiz. In the case of the sample worksheet provided above, assign 25 points for each question.

Social Studies

In our sample unit of study, the second objective for Social Studies states: Through participation in group oral presentations and written essays, students will demonstrate a basic knowledge of the history and culture of Thailand. To assess student achievement, we suggested that the teacher evaluate students' oral presentations and written essays. This could play out in the classroom in the following way.

Organize the class into teams of three students each. Assign each team to research a specific aspect of Thailand's history and culture. Sample topics could include early history, contemporary history, geography and natural resources, climate and flora/fauna, cities and country, economy, foods/diet, religion, festivals/celebrations, music, and sports. It might be helpful for the teacher to provide the students with a suggested list of approved resources to help direct students' research. Team members will write a brief essay summarizing their findings and make an oral presentation to the class.

Decide whether to evaluate each student individually or to give a team grade. The advantage of a team grade is that it generates peer pressure, encouraging each student on the team to take responsibility for the success of the project. Within each group, the students should divide up their research and work collaboratively on designing and rehearsing their presentation. In order to make sure everyone on the team is productive, tell the students that each team needs to identify what each member contributed to the presentation.

If you want to have some additional fun with this project, try making the format of the oral presentations similar to a news program. A student moderator can be assigned to interview each team. By all means, videotape or record this on a DVD if you can. Have the students dress up as if they were being interviewed on television. The tape can become part of your assessment record. Table 11.12 is a sample rubric you can use to evaluate each team's work.

Step-by-Step Outline of Activity

Objective: Through participation in group oral presentations and written essays, students will demonstrate a basic knowledge of the history and culture of Thailand.

Method of assessment: Evaluate students' oral presentations and written essays.

Scoring system: Simple rubric grid (see table 11.12).

Procedures:

1. Organize the class into teams of three students each.
2. Assign each team to research a specific aspect of Thailand's history and culture. (Sample topics could include early history, contemporary history, geography and natural resources, climate and flora/fauna, cities and country, economy, foods/diet, religion, festivals/celebrations, music, and sports.)
3. Provide a suggested list of approved resources to help direct students' research.
4. Have the members of each team work collaboratively to write a brief essay summarizing their findings.
5. Each team will share what they learned with the entire class in the form of an oral presentation.

Table 11.12. Sample Rubric for Social Studies

Objective: Through participation in group oral presentations and written essays, students will demonstrate a basic knowledge of the history and culture of Thailand.

Team: _____

Criteria

Oral Presentation	Written Essay	Teamwork
Presentation was very well organized and delivered. Points were made clearly and with substantial supporting detail.	The essay focused on the assigned topic, provided accurate information, and demonstrated very good organization.	Team members demonstrated a high level of involvement in the project.
Presentation was well organized and delivered. Most points were made clearly and with substantial supporting detail.	The essay focused on the assigned topic, provided mostly accurate information, and demonstrated good organization.	Team members demonstrated a good level of involvement in the project.
Presentation was satisfactory. Organization was average. Several points were either not made clearly or lacked substantial supporting detail.	At times, the essay focused on the assigned topic and provided accurate information; at other times, it did not. The essay demonstrated average organization.	Team members demonstrated an average level of involvement in the project.
Presentation was weak. Organization was below average. Many points were either not made clearly or lacked substantial supporting detail.	The essay did not always focus on the assigned topic or provide accurate information, and it demonstrated below average organization.	Team members demonstrated a lower than average level of involvement in the project.
Presentation was unsatisfactory. Organization was poor. Most points were not made clearly and lacked supporting detail.	The essay rarely focused on the assigned topic, provided mostly vague or inaccurate information, and demonstrated unsatisfactory organization.	Team members demonstrated an unsatisfactory level of involvement in the project.

EVALUATE THE OVERALL PROJECT

In addition to measuring student achievement, you'll want to provide ways for students, teachers, and administrators to help evaluate the project's success and to make suggestions for improvement once the show and unit of study are over. Make it clear that everyone's ideas are welcome. Solicit comments from students, colleagues, and administrators through informal conversations, debriefing meetings, surveys, and from assigned student diaries and reaction papers.

Informal Conversations

The show and unit of study will be popular topics of conversation in the halls, cafeteria, and classrooms of your school for at least a week or two afterward. You'll be part of many of these conversations and will hear people expressing their honest impressions about and reactions to the project.

Debriefing Meetings

Debriefing meetings of the various groups involved in the show and unit of study can be an effective means of getting people to discuss their experiences with the project, both positive and negative. You should hold the meetings during the week after the performance so the experience is still fresh in everyone's mind. Holding debriefing meetings can be a time saver since you will be hearing many people's views all at a specific place and time. If you hold debriefing meetings, make sure to guide the discussion so that everyone has a chance to comment on what worked well and what could be improved for the future. Take notes so that you will remember these comments and suggestions.

Surveys

Unlike informal conversations and debriefing meetings, which are usually open-ended, surveys ask participants to respond to specific questions. The following are some suggestions that may help you design a survey for the teachers involved in the project.

Include every teacher who played a role in planning and implementing the unit of study: not just the "performance" teachers (music, dance, and theatre arts) but also the classroom teachers who were involved in the project. Ask them specific questions such as:

Was sufficient time reserved for planning the unit of study together?

Were the planning sessions well organized and productive?

Were the students motivated by the activities in the unit of study?

Were the logistics and scheduling of time in the auditorium satisfactory?

You can design the survey in the form of a scale or as a series of short answers. If creating a scale, use the numbers 1 through 5, 1 being the lowest rating and 5 the highest. Teachers can circle the number that best suits their response to the question. A short answer format would allow your colleagues to write their responses to your questions using several sentences. In either case, provide a section where suggestions for improvement can be included.

If possible, invite all the participating teachers to a follow-up meeting, which you can schedule for a week or two after they have completed and returned their surveys. The purpose of this meeting would be to let everyone know that their suggestions and comments were read, to ask additional questions about their experiences, and discuss the suggestions for improvement with an eye toward the next project. You don't want people to spend time completing a survey that will be filed away and never discussed or used.

Student Diaries/Reaction Papers

Student diaries and reaction papers can be used to assess students' progress, to gain insight on the relative success of the unit of study, and to consider students' suggestions for improving the experience. The diaries can be considered formative assessments since they are written in weekly installments as the unit of study progresses. The reaction paper is written at the end of the project and can be considered a summative assessment.

At the beginning of the unit of study, teachers should tell all students involved in this project to keep regular written weekly diaries describing their experiences working on the show and/or on the unit of study. Check the students' diary books every week to make sure everyone is doing the work, and to monitor their progress.

After the performance, all students should write a reaction paper. This can be a combination of the earlier diary entries plus a new section summing up their experiences working on the project. They should support the statements they make in the reaction paper by referring to material in their diaries. Students can offer their thoughts about the success of the show or the unit of study and make constructive suggestions for improvement.

Make a Good Videotape or DVD
of the Performance

I can't overemphasize the importance of obtaining the best possible video and audio record of all your performances. No matter how busy you may be with all the details of producing the musical, always take the time to make arrangements for your shows to be recorded either on a DVD or videotape. You will get the best results if you use a professional sound engineer. Explain to your principal that it is important for assessment purposes as well as for the school's archives to get the best possible recording made. After your first musical, include these expenses in the budget request you make to your principal for the following years. If your school truly can't afford this expense, try to find a teacher or parent who is skilled at doing this and who has good equipment.

In hindsight, it would have been great if I had paid more attention to getting the best possible video and audio recordings made of the middle school musicals I produced. Unfortunately, we waited until the last minute to make arrangements and ended up with a crew of unsupervised students using mediocre school equipment. The students did their best, but the resulting recordings were not very good, and I regret that. You can avoid a similar situation with some advance planning. Remember that while it is okay to use your recordings for educational purposes, it is not permissible to use them for commercial purposes or fundraising.

FOR THE FUTURE

The information in this chapter should help you find ways to assess the success of your performance and unit of study. Share these ideas with teachers in other subject areas who are involved in the project. You should all be able to explain how you plan to evaluate the project. This will lend a greater sense of academic legitimacy to the entire endeavor.

ASSESSMENT AS ADVOCACY

Up to this point, we have discussed how assessment can help measure student achievement and gauge the effectiveness of your unit of study. In addition, assessment can be a powerful tool for advocacy once you can demonstrate that you've gone through an evaluation process. There is no substitute for written or recorded evidence showing the value of what you've done!

Later on, if you ever need to justify your program or demonstrate a good reason to expand your program to parents, administrators, or a school board, you can prepare an advocacy package including excerpts from student diaries and reaction papers, the teacher surveys, and the performance DVD or videotape as evidence of the quality of your project. You will then be well equipped to make the argument that studying and performing musicals in the middle school can be a valuable teaching tool that makes learning exciting for everyone in the school community!

REFERENCES

Askew, J. M., Persky, H. R., and Sandene, B. A. (1998). *The National Assessment of Educational Progress 1997 Arts Report Card*. Washington, DC: United States Department of Education Office of Educational Research and Improvement.

Bobetsky, V. (2005). "Arranging Musicals for Middle School Voices." *Teaching Music*, 12(4), 34–40.

Consortium of National Arts Education Associations. (1994). *National Standards for Arts Education*. Reston, VA: MENC.

Dewey, J. (1938). *Experience and Education*. New York: Macmillan.

Hammerstein, O., and Rodgers, R. (1951). *The King and I*. New York: Random House.

Hinckley, J., and Shull, S. (1996). *Strategies for Teaching Middle-Level General Music*. Lanham, MD: Rowman & Littlefield.

Landon, M. M. (1943). *Anna and the King of Siam*. New York: John Day and Company.

Leonowens, A. H. (1870). *The English Governess at the Siamese Court*. Boston: Fields, Osgood and Company.

National Council for the Social Studies. (1994). *Expectations of Excellence: Curriculum Standards for Social Studies*. Waldorf, MD: National Council for the Social Studies.

National Council of Teachers of English and the International Reading Association. (1996). *Standards for the English Language Arts*. Urbana, IL: National Council of Teachers of English.

Robertson, C. (2006). "They Get to Put On a Show in the Bronx." *New York Times*, May 10, E3.

Soeby, L. M. (1991). *Way Off Broadway*. Jefferson, NC: Mc Farland and Company.

Spolin, V. (1963). *Improvisation for the Theater: A Handbook of Teaching and Directing Techniques*. Evanston, IL: Northwestern University Press.

Spolin, V. (1986). *Theatre Games for the Classroom: A Teacher's Handbook*. Evanston, IL: Northwestern University Press.

ABOUT THE AUTHOR

Victor V. Bobetsky is associate professor of music education at Hunter College, where he directs the teacher education program in music. His degrees include a BA in music from Brooklyn College, an MA in music from Hunter College, and a doctor of musical arts in piano performance from the University of Miami, Florida. Dr. Bobetsky began his career in music education as the choral director at Junior High School 51 in Brooklyn, New York, where he directed the annual spring musical. He went on to supervise K–12 music and arts teachers in Columbus, Ohio, West Hartford, Connecticut, and East Meadow, New York. Dr. Bobetsky's choral arrangements for middle school voices are published by Boosey and Hawkes, Cambiata Press, GIA Publications, and Musica Russica.

Breinigsville, PA USA
17 October 2010
247494BV00001B/1/P